STRONG REPROOFS *for a* SCANDALOUS CHURCH

A STUDY OF 1 CORINTHIANS 1:1–6:11

BIBLE STUDY GUIDE

From the Bible-teaching ministry of

Charles R. Swindoll

INSIGHT FOR LIVING

Charles R. Swindoll is a graduate of Dallas Theological Seminary and has served in pastorates for more than twenty-four years, including churches in Texas, New England, and California. Since 1971 he has served as senior pastor of the First Evangelical Free Church of Fullerton, California. Chuck's radio program, "Insight for Living," began in 1979. In addition to his church and radio ministries, Chuck has written twenty-three books and numerous booklets on a variety of subjects.

This guide is the first in a three-part series on the book of 1 Corinthians. Based on the outlines of Chuck's sermons, the study guide text is coauthored by Julie Martin, a graduate of Biola University. The Living Insights are written by Bill Butterworth, a graduate of Florida Bible College, Dallas Theological Seminary, and Florida Atlantic University. Julie Martin is an associate editor in the Educational Products Department at Insight for Living, and Bill Butterworth is currently a staff writer in the Educational Products Department.

Editor in Chief:	Cynthia Swindoll
Coauthor of Text:	Julie Martin
Author of Living Insights:	Bill Butterworth
Copy Manager:	Jac La Tour
Senior Copy Editor:	Jane Gillis
Copy Editor:	Wendy Peterson
Director, Communications Division:	Carla Beck
Project Manager:	Nina Paris
Project Supervisor:	Cassandra Clark
Art Director:	Donna Mayo
Production Artists:	Wanda Roberts and Diana Vasquez
Typographer:	Bob Haskins
Cover Photographer:	Tom Grill/Comstock Inc.
Print Production Manager:	Deedee Snyder
Printer:	Frye and Smith

Unless otherwise identified, all Scripture references are from the New American Standard Bible, © The Lockman Foundation 1960, 1962, 1963, 1968, 1971, 1972, 1973, 1975, 1977. Used by permission.

ISBN 0-8499-8298-7

Ordering Information

An album that contains twelve messages on six cassettes and corresponds to this study guide may be purchased through the Sales Department of Insight for Living, Post Office Box 4444, Fullerton, California 92634. For ordering information and a current catalog, please write our office or call (714) 870-9161.

Canadian residents may obtain a catalog and ordering information through Insight for Living Ministries, Post Office Box 2510, Vancouver, British Columbia, Canada V6B 3W7, (604) 272-5811. Australian residents should direct their correspondence to Insight for Living Ministries, General Post Office Box 2823 EE, Melbourne, Victoria 3001. Other overseas residents should direct their correspondence to our Fullerton office.

If you wish to order by Visa or MasterCard, you are welcome to use our toll-free number, (800) 772-8888, Monday through Friday, between the hours of 8:30 A.M. and 4:00 P.M., Pacific time. This number may be used anywhere in the United States except Alaska, California, and Hawaii. Orders from these areas can be made by calling our general office number, (714) 870-9161. Orders from Canada can be made by calling (604) 272-5811.

Table of Contents

Strong Reproofs
for a Scandalous Church
A Study of 1 Corinthians 1:1–6:11

Corinth . . . century-one Corinth. What a mess! Fast and gaudy, shallow and brassy, slick and sassy, sensual and busy Corinth. The Vanity Fair of ancient Greece. A sailor's favorite port. A prodigal's paradise. A policeman's nightmare. A preacher's graveyard.

Until Paul came along. A clash was inevitable. When the straight-and-narrow truth of the gospel confronted the loose-and-permissive carnality of Corinth, the expected occurred. The truth won out, however, as God's Word stood the test and an assembly of believers emerged, forming a church in Corinth that Paul planted, Apollos watered, and God blessed.

It wasn't long, however, before the little, newly formed church began to bear the marks of the surrounding Corinthian lifestyle. Carnality resulted in scandal, as the Corinthian Christians substituted human intellect for divine wisdom, which led their founder to write this letter of strong reproof. As we begin this study of 1 Corinthians, let's realize that if such things could happen in the first century, they could certainly happen in the twentieth.

May God's reproofs retain their impact today!

Chuck Swindoll

Putting Truth into Action

Knowledge apart from application falls short of God's desire for His children. Knowledge must result in change and growth. Consequently, we have constructed this Bible study guide with these purposes in mind: (1) to stimulate discovery, (2) to increase understanding, and (3) to encourage application.

At the end of each lesson is a section called ▨ Living Insights. There you'll be given assistance in further Bible study, and you'll be encouraged to contemplate and apply the things you've learned. This is the place where the lesson is fitted with shoe leather for your walk through the varied experiences of life.

It's our hope that you'll discover numerous ways to use this tool. Some useful avenues we suggest are personal meditation, joint discovery, and discussion with your spouse, family, work associates, friends, or neighbors. The study guide is also practical for Sunday school classes, Bible study groups, and, of course, as a study aid for the "Insight for Living" radio broadcast.

In order to derive the greatest benefit from this process, we suggest that you record your responses to the lessons in the space which has been provided for you. In view of the kinds of questions asked, your study guide may become a journal filled with your many discoveries and commitments. We anticipate that you will find yourself returning to it periodically for review and encouragement.

Julie Martin
Coauthor of Text

Bill Butterworth
Author of Living Insights

STRONG REPROOFS *for a* SCANDALOUS CHURCH

A STUDY OF 1 CORINTHIANS 1:1–6:11

Once Corinthians, Now Californians

Acts 18:1–11, 1 Corinthians

Driving around San Francisco with eyes glued to a map, most first-time tourists don't see much. When they're not trying to make sense of the city's layout, it's all they can do to survive the streets—those one-way, ever-winding roller coaster roads. Like a mouse in a maze, they'll more than likely have to take a few wrong turns and bump into a few dead ends before getting to the prize—the Golden Gate Bridge or Fisherman's Wharf or Lombard Street.

But what if all those wishing to tour San Francisco were first given a helicopter view of the city? What if they were able to look at the logic of its layout from above the fog? Then it would make sense. And once back on the city's streets, they'd be able to find their way.

Before trolleying through the streets of 1 Corinthians, we need first to get a bird's-eye view of its twists and turns; we will ignore the trees and look only at the forest. As we do, we will see that Corinth was much like California today—drunk on wealth and immorality, one of the vice capitals of the world. And we will be able to take Paul's message of rebuke to heart, for, like the Corinthians, we are members of a godless society in desperate need of the transforming message of Jesus.

I. The City of Corinth

So we won't get lost, let's take time to get an overall perspective of this ancient city.

> Corinth, perched like a one-eyed Titan astride the narrow isthmus connecting the Greek mainland with the Peloponnese, was one of the dominant commercial centers of the Hellenic world.[1]

Corinth's location was the key to its opulence. The city controlled access to two seas, the Aegean in the west and the Ionian in the east.

---

1. "Introduction: 1 Corinthians," in *The NIV Study Bible* (Grand Rapids, Mich.: Zondervan Bible Publishers, 1985), p. 1733.

Travelers and traders could enter Corinth through one of its two harbors, Lechaeum and Cenchrea, or through the north-south land route the city governed. Goods poured into its gates from every country imaginable, making Corinth—the Vanity Fair of Greece—an extremely wealthy, populous, and pluralistic city. Corinth was, however, also a center of vice. The Corinthians worshiped many gods and goddesses, the most famous being Aphrodite—the goddess of love. A thousand prostitutes served in her temple by day, swarming onto the streets at night. Corinth's reputation for sexual promiscuity was so widespread that a term was coined to describe it: *to Corinthianize,* meaning "to practice sexual immorality." Corinth was also the site of the Isthmian Games, which were second in importance only to the Olympics. The Isthmian contests were held every two years and lasted several days. Athletic, equestrian, and musical competitions were conducted in Corinth's huge stadium as well as its two theaters—one outdoors that seated eighteen thousand people and another indoors that held three thousand. These games were not only popular but also known for their extravagance and licentiousness. Even in sports, Corinth lived up to its infamous name.[2]

II. Paul's Visit (Acts 18)

Paul traveled to Corinth around A.D. 51, his zeal to spread the gospel stronger than any fear he might have had over the city's reputation. He met two fellow Jews there, Aquila and his wife Priscilla, who had recently left Italy because the emperor Claudius had ordered all Jews out of Rome (v. 2). Drawn together by their Jewish heritage and common trade of tentmaking, Paul stayed with them and discipled them, preaching in the synagogue every Sabbath "trying to persuade Jews and Greeks" (v. 4). When Silas and Timothy came, Paul relied on their support, leaving his trade and concentrating his efforts on the Jews (v. 5). But the Jews were hostile and blasphemous, so Paul left them and focused his ministry on the Gentiles, many of whom believed and were baptized (vv. 6–8). Despite this success, Paul apparently still felt afraid and depressed (v. 9).

> In Paul's mind, ... a seed of worry took root, that the pattern of previous cities was about to be repeated: rejection by Jews, progress among the pagans, fury from Jews, expulsion by mob violence or judicial process just when the gospel gained a hold. ... The depression which was one of the strands of Paul's nature seemed to gain the

2. More information on Corinth may be found in these sources: *Jesus and Paul: Places They Knew,* by F. F. Bruce (Nashville, Tenn.: Thomas Nelson Publishers, 1983), pp. 101–5; "1 Corinthians," by Harold Mare in *The Expositor's Bible Commentary,* 12 vols., ed. Frank E. Gaebelein (Grand Rapids, Mich.: Zondervan Publishing House, 1976), vol. 10, pp. 175–79; *Archaeology in Bible Lands,* by Howard F. Vos (Chicago, Ill.: Moody Press, 1977), pp. 354–56.

upper hand. He would never win another Corinthian to Christ, see the sparkle of new life in a man's eyes. And he dreaded the physical agony of another stoning or a beating with rods; the desolation of being flung out again with winter now on them, the seas turbulent, and nowhere to take his stiff, aging joints but the mountain trails of the Peloponnesus.[3]

Jesus comforted Paul in a vision, rallying his spirits with these words:

"Do not be afraid any longer, but go on speaking and do not be silent; for I am with you, and no man will attack you in order to harm you, for I have many people in this city." (vv. 9–10)

So Paul stayed on in Corinth for more than eighteen months (vv. 11, 18a), his heart becoming welded to the Corinthians as he watched them come to Christ and slowly grow in their faith. The Lord was truly faithful.

Paul: An Example to Imitate

Corinth attracted a potpourri of people—from athletes and merchants to gangsters and prostitutes. But before Paul came, the city lacked a preacher of righteousness, someone to guide them through the confusing streets of life. Probably, others were intimidated by the decadent city and didn't dare make it their mission field. But Paul came in and faithfully directed the Corinthians' hearts toward Jesus.

Like Paul, are you willing to lead the lost around you? Are you sharing with others the map to salvation and abundant living, or are you keeping it hidden? I encourage you to shine your light . . . share the answer . . . point the way to Jesus (see Matt. 5:14–16).

In the autumn of A.D. 52, Paul left Corinth with Aquila and Priscilla and set sail for Ephesus (Acts 18:18b–19a). He left his friends there and traveled on to Caesarea and Antioch before beginning another missionary journey (vv. 19–22). While Aquila and Priscilla worked and witnessed in Ephesus, they heard a Jew named Apollos boldly sharing what little he knew about Jesus (vv. 24–26a). They took him aside and filled in the blanks of his knowledge, so that when he left Ephesus for Corinth, he was able to effectively build on the foundation Paul had patiently laid (18:26b–19:1). While Apollos served in Corinth, Paul returned to Ephesus and began to correspond with the Corinthian church.

---

3. John Pollock, *The Man Who Shook the World* (Wheaton, Ill.: Victor Books, 1972), p. 124.

III. The Corinthian Correspondence

Before moving on to the specifics of the letter, let's first get a grip on its background and layout.

A. Its background. The first letter Paul wrote to Corinth, mentioned in 1 Corinthians 5:9, has been lost. According to Paul, the Corinthian believers misunderstood this letter (vv. 10–13), so to clear up the confusion, he wrote them the epistle we know as 1 Corinthians. Another reason Paul penned this second letter was to address a number of problems that were dividing and disorienting the church. He heard about these difficulties from Chloe's household and a three-man delegation sent by the Corinthians (1:11, 16:17). Paul tells the believers:

> Now I exhort you, brethren, by the name of our Lord Jesus Christ, that you all agree, and there be no divisions among you, but you be made complete in the same mind and in the same judgment. For I have been informed concerning you, my brethren, by Chloe's people, that there are quarrels among you. (vv. 10–11)

A Checkpoint for Gossip

One of the best ways to end a rumor is to ask if you may quote the individual passing it along. If the person says no, it's possible that the rumor is just idle talk. If the person answers yes, you should contact the gossip's subject to verify the story you heard.

Also, if you like to spread news about others, ask yourself if you would want someone to quote you. A negative answer is a good sign you should keep your lips sealed on the matter. And a positive response should lead not to back-fence reporting but to up-front confronting.

B. Its layout. Written about A.D. 55, 1 Corinthians has four main sections: an introduction (1:1–9), a series of rebukes for sin (1:10–6:20), a number of replies to questions (7:1–16:12), and a conclusion (16:13–24). The letter is filled with practical solutions to problems in the pews. The central thrust of the epistle is summed up in the closing exhortation: "Be on the alert, stand firm in the faith, act like men, be strong. Let all that you do be done in love" (vv. 13–14).

The Letters of Our Lives

Our lives are like 1 Corinthians. They have an introduction to the fleshly life that begins in our mother's womb. And they also have a conclusion. One day, our earthly lives

---

will come to an end, and their postscripts will be found in the obituaries.

The real message of this letter is for those whose conclusion is unsure. There's something much worse than being lost in the streets of San Francisco. And that's being lost in the streets of life. Without a guide, life offers nothing but tangled, snaking roads and street signs hidden by the fog.

There is one—the light of the world, Jesus Christ—who will beacon the darkest streets of your life if you will just put away your map and let Him lead the way.

"I am the way, and the truth, and the life; no one comes to the Father, but through Me." (John 14:6; see also 1:9, 3:16)

 Living Insights

Study One

We're off to a good start in our study of *Strong Reproofs*. It's important to understand the background of a book in order to grasp its contents. Let's do a little overviewing so we can get a feel for this letter as an entire unit.

- Block out some time to skim through 1 Corinthians. If you can't get through the whole book in one sitting, just read through the first six chapters. Using the following chart, jot down observations that tie into the title *Strong Reproofs for a Scandalous Church.* You'll be amazed at how much material relates to this theme.

Strong Reproofs for a Scandalous Church	
Verses	Observations

Continued on next page

Verses	Observations

Living Insights

Study Two

Any wise traveler goes through a series of preparatory steps before embarking on a journey. In a sense, we are also embarking on a journey—a spiritual journey. Are you adequately prepared for your trek?

- Using the space provided, write down your thoughts about your lifestyle. Does it reflect a readiness to learn new spiritual truths? What can you do to prepare your heart for this study? Are there any hindrances you need to talk to God about? Jot down your thoughts and conclude with a time of prayer. Ask God to give you special insights throughout this study.

Preparation for My Spiritual Journey

_____

_____

_____

_____

_____

_____

_____

_____

_____

_____

1 Corinthians: A Survey

Writer: Paul (1:1, 16:21)
Place of writing: Ephesus (16:8)

Recipients: Christians in Corinth (1:2)
Background: Acts 18:1–18a

Date: Approximately A.D. 57
Theme: "Christian Conduct in the Local Church"

Introduction	Rebuke for Sinful Conditions (1:10–6:20) Key: "Now I exhort you, brethren . . ." (1:10a)			Reply to Specific Questions (7:1–16:9) Key: "Now concerning the things about which you wrote . . ." (7:1a)						Conclusion
	Divisions	Disorders		Domestic	Social	Ecclesiastical	Practical	Doctrinal	Financial	
						Difficulties				
	Exposed 1:10–17	Moral 5:1–13		Marriage and Divorce	Liberty and License	Women and Worship	Gifts and Body	Death and Resurrection	Giving and Receiving	
	Explained 1:18–4:5	Legal 6:1–11								
	Applied 4:6–21	Carnal 6:12–20								
1:1–9	1:10–4:21	5:1–6:20		7:1–40	8:1–11:1	11:2–34	12:1–14:40	15:1–58	16:1–9	16:10–24

7

From Riches to Rags
1 Corinthians 1:1–9

The life of Edgar Allan Poe is one of the most tragic of all American writers. Within a brief span of forty years he literally went from riches to rags. Raised by foster parents who loved him deeply, he was provided with an education that matched his genius in his field of interest. He attended private schools in England. He was schooled in Richmond at the University of Virginia. He even spent a period of time as a cadet at West Point.

Poe, in his heyday, was unparalleled as a literary critic, editor, poet, and author of short stories. Most of us have probably had our spines tingled by *The Pit and the Pendulum* or *The Tell-Tale Heart* or *The Raven.* His works have indeed left their mark.

But the mark left by his life is another story. Poe lost his young bride through a bitter case of tuberculosis. By that time, alcohol and drug abuse, along with involvement in the occult and Satanism, had proved to be his undoing. Depression and insanity plagued his short life, eventually leaving him unconscious in the gutter of a windswept street in Baltimore. Four days later he died, having never regained consciousness.

Poe began his life with money and brilliance, which quickly brought him prestige and fame. But it was only a matter of time before he became a ragged, penniless bum.

This tragedy—the slow slip from riches to rags—happens not only to individuals but to churches as well. The church at Corinth was just such a case. Its beginning was so rich that it seemed invincible. Like Poe, it went from riches to the beggarly rags of spiritual poverty before it finally ended up in the gutter.

In the letter of 1 Corinthians Paul addresses the impoverished spiritual condition of this church and tells how to be restored to spiritual wealth.

I. The Writer and His Companion
Paul identifies himself in the opening of this letter, reminding the Corinthians of his position.

Paul, called as an apostle of Jesus Christ by the will of God. (v. 1a)

The Corinthians obviously knew that Paul was an apostle. So why did he remind them? Because only a person with such authority would be able to bring the rebukes, the words of admonition, the severe criticism he was about to bring—and have them accepted. The fact that Paul was an apostle meant four things. First, he had received his commission directly from the Savior. The Lord appeared to him and declared him ordained of God (Acts 9:15). Second, he

8

had seen the resurrected Christ with his own eyes. A persecutor of Christians, Paul, then called Saul, was confronted by Jesus on the road to Damascus and was saved on that same day (vv. 1–19). Third, he had supreme authority to perform miracles at will. He had power to heal, to discern good and evil, to speak boldly and without error (v. 22). Fourth, he answered to no man, only to God. There was a healthy independence about Paul. Having God's favor was more important to him than enjoying the favor of men (see Gal. 1:10).[1] Paul also includes "Sosthenes our brother" in his introduction. The exact identification of Sosthenes is unknown; however, most Bible scholars believe he was the *amanuensis,* the one who actually penned Paul's words as he dictated them. What we do know from the phrase "our brother" is that Sosthenes was familiar to the Corinthian believers, was Paul's friend, and most likely agreed with the content of his letter.[2]

II. The Recipients

Next, Paul identifies the recipients of his letter.

> To the church of God which is at Corinth, to those who have been sanctified in Christ Jesus, saints by calling, with all who in every place call upon the name of our Lord Jesus Christ, their Lord and ours: Grace to you and peace from God our Father and the Lord Jesus Christ. (vv. 2–3)

A. Who they are. First Corinthians is addressed to the church. The Greek word is *ekklēsia,* meaning "called out." The church is not brick and mortar, stained glass and padded pews, but the body of people saved through faith in Christ. When Christians gather for worship, the buildings merely house the church. But when we go our separate ways, the church goes with us— because we *are* the church. Paul also addressed them as sanctified, which means "set apart by God to be his holy people."[3] Sanctification isn't something that comes and goes; it isn't dependent on our actions. Sanctification is a position in Christ. It's how God sees us. Holy. Set apart. Paul also gives his recipients a third title: saints. *Saint* means "devoted, consecrated, pure, holy." In God's eyes we are cleansed, uniquely marked as His.

---

1. For a complete definition of *apostle,* see *Word Meanings in the New Testament,* by Ralph Earle (Grand Rapids, Mich.: Baker Book House, 1986), p. 236.

2. If you're interested in discovering more about the mysterious Sosthenes, see *The First Epistle to the Corinthians,* by C. K. Barrett (New York, N.Y.: Harper and Row, 1968), p. 30; and *First Corinthians,* by Robert B. Hughes (Chicago, Ill.: Moody Press, 1985), pp. 24–25.

3. F. F. Bruce, ed., *1 and 2 Corinthians* (Greenwood, S.C.: Attic Press, 1971), p. 30.

B. Where they live. Paul addresses this letter to "the church of God which is at Corinth." There was nothing spiritually significant about the city of Corinth. It was a city like many others. The point is that you don't need to live in a particular place to walk with Christ. All saints are equally set apart by God as His children; therefore, all are related as members of God's worldwide family. Our identity is not with a city or a certain preacher but with Jesus Christ.

C. What they need. In verse 3, Paul reveals the desire he had for the Corinthians.

Grace to you and peace from God our Father and the Lord Jesus Christ.

Aware of the church's divisiveness, he greets them with the desire that they would experience grace and peace—two virtues needed to keep a church in harmony. Paul wanted the Corinthians to be known as gracious saints who lived at peace with one another.

┌─ *Virtue Check* ─────────────────────────

How gracious are you as God's child? How kind? How compassionate? How quick to forgive? Think of the grace and peace God has given you through the gift of His Son. You can never repay Him for these free gifts, but you can thank Him by passing them along to others.

And be kind to one another, tender-hearted, forgiving each other, just as God in Christ also has forgiven you. (Eph. 4:32)

III. The Corinthians' Riches

Before trying to remove the spots from the Corinthians' spiritual clothing, Paul recalls their strengths and blessings.[4]

> I thank my God always concerning you, for the grace of God which was given you in Christ Jesus, that in everything you were enriched in Him, in all speech and all knowledge, even as the testimony concerning Christ was confirmed in you, so that you are not lacking in any gift, awaiting eagerly the revelation of our Lord Jesus Christ. (vv. 4–7)

Looking for Gold

"Paul looks at the Corinthian church as it is *in Christ* before he looks at anything else that is true of the church. That disciplined statement of faith is rarely made in local churches. The warts are examined and lamented, but often there is no vision of what God has already done in Christ. If the first nine verses of this letter were excised from the text, it would be impossible for any reader to come to anything but a fairly pessimistic view of the church at Corinth. The statements of faith, hope and love that occur at frequent intervals in the text would have no context; they would degenerate into pious dreams."[5]

Do you let the flaws, weaknesses, and vulnerabilities of others blind you to the strengths and blessings? Or when you see the dark side, do you remember that somewhere underneath the tarnish there still lies shining gold?

A. Genuinely saved. The basis of gratitude is grace—the goodness God lavishes on us even though we could never earn or repay it.

> I thank my God always concerning you, for the grace of God which was given you in Christ Jesus. (v. 4)

In spite of our rebellion against Him, He loves us (Rom. 5:8). He continues to offer us what we need even when we shove it back in His face. The Corinthians had experienced God's grace, receiving His gift of salvation by trusting in His Son.

B. Generously endowed. The Corinthians had also been endowed with eloquent, sound teaching.

---

4. For a discussion on the importance of synchronous blessing and discipline, see *The Blessing,* by Gary Smalley and John Trent (Nashville, Tenn.: Thomas Nelson Publishers, 1986), pp. 104–7.

5. David Prior, *The Message of 1 Corinthians: Life in the Local Church* (Downers Grove, Ill.: InterVarsity Press, 1985), p. 23.

> That in everything you were enriched in Him, in all
> speech and all knowledge. (v. 5)

"All speech and all knowledge" refers to all forms of teaching and admonition—theoretical and practical, didactic and devotional. This was the wealth of teaching and knowledge the Corinthians enjoyed under Paul and Apollos.

C. Securely established. The Corinthians were blessed in another way: their lives were firmly rooted in the gospel.

> Even as the testimony concerning Christ was con-
> firmed in you. (v. 6)

Confirmed means "established, made sure, stable." They were faithfully instructed to the point that they became stable in their understanding of the gospel.

D. Spiritually gifted. When it came to spiritual gifts, the Corinthians had it all.

> So that you are not lacking in any gift. (v. 7a)

"So that" refers to a result. Because they were fully nourished on the best of biblical diets, they lacked no gift (see 12:4–11).

You Are What You Eat

How's *your* spiritual health? Is your walk with God sluggish from ingesting the doughnuts and coffee, potato chips and soda of society's snack shops? Or are you spiritually energetic, table spread with the whole wheat and honey of God's Word?

E. Prophetically alert. Verse 7 concludes:

> Awaiting eagerly the revelation of our Lord Jesus
> Christ.

The Corinthians knew His coming was near. They knew eternity was on its way. And they lived in anxious anticipation of the day when they would see His face (compare Rom. 8:19, 23; Phil. 3:20).

IV. The Rewards

After reminding the Corinthians of their riches, Paul names two rewards given them as saints—rewards we as saints can claim as our own. The first one deals with our future.

> Who shall also confirm you to the end, blameless in the
> day of our Lord Jesus Christ. (v. 8)

In eternity, we will be *blameless,* which means "unimpeachable." God's saints will never be indicted by either the angels or the Trinity—we will be brought into eternity blameless. The second reward can be enjoyed while we wait.

God is faithful, through whom you were called into fellowship with His Son, Jesus Christ our Lord. (v. 9)

Not only will we spend eternity with Jesus, but we can enjoy fellowship with Him right now.

V. Principles to Practice

We're a lot like the Corinthians—elected, enriched, established in
Christ. But there is one important difference. *We* have the opportu-
nity to study the lives of the ancient churches and learn the easy
way of holding on to the blessings Christ has given us . . . of how not
to let sin turn our riches into rags. In review, let's recall four principles that can be gleaned from this lesson—principles that, if re-
membered, will keep our spiritual garments from becoming ragged.

**A. No wrongs or weaknesses should take away our grat-
itude for others.** Every one of us is flawed. But rather than
reject each other because of our weaknesses, we need to be
thankful for each other. Remember—the Lord is at work in us
all, removing our imperfections, until one day we all will stand
spotless before Him.

**B. The basis of any praiseworthy thing we have or do is
grace.** The Corinthians were rich only because of what God
had done in their lives. Likewise, grace and grace alone has
brought us where we are (see Eph. 1:7–8a, 2:8–9).

**C. A rich, impressive beginning is no guarantee of the
same kind of ending.** We all know the saying, The bigger
they are, the harder they fall. Satan has a similar motto: The
bigger they *think* they are, the harder they fall (see Prov. 16:18).
The Corinthians let their spiritual health go to their heads and
were knocked to the canvas by their own pride. As believers
graciously endowed with good gifts, we need to guard our hearts
from pride, careful always to give God the glory.

**D. No degree of carnality or failure can ever remove our
blameless acceptance in God's presence.** Even after
trading their riches for rags, the Corinthians, remarkably, re-
mained blameless in God's eyes (compare Rom. 8:1). Regardless
of how carnal, those Corinthians were cradled so securely in
Christ's hands that even Satan could not snatch them away
(John 10:28). Whether you're walking with the Lord and enjoying
the riches of His blessings or groveling around ragged in life's
gutter, cling to the cross . . . hold on to His promises.

> **"And Can It Be?"**
> And can it be that I should gain
> An int'rest in the Savior's blood?
> Died He for me, who caused His pain?

13

For me, who Him to death pursued?
Amazing love! how can it be
That Thou, my God shouldst die for me?

No condemnation now I dread:
Jesus, and all in Him, is mine!
Alive in Him, my living Head,
And clothed in righteousness divine,
Bold I approach th'eternal throne,
And claim the crown, thru Christ my own.[6]

 Living Insights

Study One ▬▬▬▬▬▬▬▬▬▬▬▬▬▬▬▬▬▬▬▬▬▬

Many great spiritual truths have been stated in the text we've been studying. We've been referring to them as "riches" in this lesson. Let's invest some additional time in researching these riches.

● Read through 1 Corinthians 1:1–9. Write down the key words of this passage. With the assistance of a Bible dictionary, create a concise definition for each term. Then finish up by writing down a sentence explaining why that word is significant.

1 Corinthians 1:1–9

Key word: _____

Definition: _____   Significance: _____

_____   _____

_____   _____

Key word: _____

Definition: _____   Significance: _____

_____   _____

_____   _____

---

6. Charles Wesley, "And Can It Be?" in *The Hymnal for Worship and Celebration* (Waco, Tex.: Word Music, 1986), no. 203.

14

Key word: _____

Definition: _____ Significance: _____

_____ _____

_____ _____

Key word: _____

Definition: _____ Significance: _____

_____ _____

_____ _____

Key word: _____

Definition: _____ Significance: _____

_____ _____

_____ _____

Key word: _____

Definition: _____ Significance: _____

_____ _____

_____ _____

Key word: _____

Definition: _____ Significance: _____

_____ _____

_____ _____

Key word: _____

Definition: _____ Significance: _____

_____ _____

_____ _____

Key word: _____

Definition: _____ Significance: _____

_____ _____

_____ _____

Continued on next page

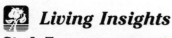 *Living Insights*

The basis of anything we have or do that's worthy of praise is God's grace. If you ponder that statement long enough, your gratitude to the Lord can't help but increase.

● How is God's grace being evidenced in your life? Certainly there are examples from your past—but there are probably some illustrations from your present that you may be overlooking. Use the space provided to list some of the demonstrations of God's grace in your life.

Evidences of God's Grace in My Life

_____

_____

_____

_____

_____

_____

_____

_____

_____

_____

_____

_____

_____

_____

_____

_____

_____

_____

_____

_____

How to Split a Church

1 Corinthians 1:10–17

Divorce used to be spoken of in the most hushed of tones . . . it was a dark and secret thing that happened only to a distant relative or the mean neighbor down the street. But now it's a household word. Many of us have felt the devastating fallout from this cruel bomb. Debris from the impact of two colliding wills flies indiscriminately and often lands on the most innocent—the children.

Most marriages begin with lace and white satin, honeymoon suites and gifts, ribbons and bows on the threshold. But if husband and wife quit cleaving to each other, the wedding gown soon yellows, the cake's frosting bitters, and the wedding bells begin to toll death's dirge.

Like the breakup of a marriage, so a congregational divorce is painful and tragic—especially for babes in the Lord who look to their spiritual parents for security and nurturing.

The church at Corinth was about to experience such a divorce. Their unified body was becoming nothing more than a hodgepodge of separate parts, each pursuing its own desires. What was it that threatened to split and tear the bond the Corinthian congregation once thrived under? What was turning their harmony to dissonance . . . their commitment to divisiveness . . . their dreams to nightmares?

Paul knew. He saw the cracks in their unity. He knew that the church would soon split, so he wrote a letter encouraging the Corinthians to reconcile—to leave their selfish desires and renew their vows of commitment by cleaving to each other in the Lord Jesus.

I. Paul's Exhortation

"Now I exhort[1] you, brethren," begins Paul (1 Cor. 1:10a). In addressing the Corinthians as "brethren," Paul approaches them tenderly, as if drawing them together for a family counsel. Yet his words also carry the strength of God, as he exhorts them "by the name of our Lord Jesus Christ." Compelled by his love for them and using his authority to speak in Christ's name, Paul urges these believers to tear up the divorce papers and be united once again.

A. Negative. He urges the Corinthians to have "no divisions among [them]" (v. 10). *Divisions* comes from the word *schisma,* meaning "to separate, to rip, to tear, to split." This body Paul has loved and nurtured is now ruptured, broken, divided; and he is deeply concerned.

---

1. The Greek word for *exhort* is *parakaleō,* meaning "to call alongside." It conveys the idea of encouraging and helping someone get back on the right track.

B. Positive. Paul also encourages them to "all agree" and "be made complete[2] in the same mind and in the same judgment" (v. 10b). He wants the Corinthians to have an attitude of flexibility and oneness. They were all doing what was right in their own eyes, creating an obnoxious cacophony, and Paul wanted them to tune in to the Spirit and live in harmony.

> ### Harmony in Diversity
> An orchestra full of tubas playing only the tuba score would be monotonous—it could never create the beautiful chords that strike our hearts so deeply. So, too, God's congregational orchestras need all the different instruments playing the full score in order to produce a rich, harmonious sound, pleasing to His ears (see 1 Cor. 12:17–18, Eph. 4:15–16).

II. The Corinthians' Situation

In verses 11–15, Paul moves from generalities to pointed specifics. Basing his admonition on the account he received from "Chloe's people," he addresses this church's many problems.

A. Their quarrels. First on Paul's list is the frequent squabbling among these believers.

> For I have been informed concerning you, my brethren, by Chloe's people, that there are quarrels among you. (v. 11)

Notice that the apostle does not blame Satan for their quarreling. We frequently forget that our fleshly natures often pull sin's pin without Satan's prompting and give him the credit for the explosion. Instead, Paul lays the blame at the Corinthians' feet, pointing out that their spiritual immaturity was creating the fireworks.

> And I, brethren, could not speak to you as to spiritual men, but as to men of flesh, as to babes in Christ. I gave you milk to drink, not solid food; for you were not yet able to receive it. Indeed, even now you are not yet able, for you are still fleshly. For since there is jealousy and strife among you, are you not fleshly, and are you not walking like mere men? (3:1–3)

---

2. To *complete* "literally means 'put in order, restore . . . restore to its former condition.' . . . It is used of fishermen 'mending' their nets (Matt. 4:21; Mark 1:19). . . . Here in Corinthians it means 'make one what he ought to be.' . . . The idea is that of being *'fitted together,* as the fragments in a piece of mosaic, in which each minute portion exactly fills its proper place.' " From *Word Meanings in the New Testament,* by Ralph Earle (Grand Rapids, Mich.: Baker Book House, 1986), p. 215.

B. Their cliques. Paul names four factions that were tearing the
Corinthian church apart (1 Cor. 1:12).

   1. The Paul party. Paul ministered to the Gentiles; in fact, it
was from Paul's lips that they first heard the good news
about liberty in Christ. It's possible that this was the group
who was becoming licentious, turning grace into a green
light for the flesh. Whether or not these Paulites were the
ones who took advantage of grace, we don't know; but we
do know that their devotion to Paul was based on his bringing the light of the gospel to their dark, pagan lives.

   2. The Apollos party. After Paul left the church at Corinth,
Apollos arrived and "helped greatly those who had believed
through grace; for he powerfully refuted the Jews in public,
demonstrating by the Scriptures that Jesus was the Christ"
(Acts 18:27b–28). Apollos was intellectually and scripturally
astute, as well as an eloquent preacher. Greeks especially
would have been drawn to him since they were enamored
of rhetorical and argumentative skills. Paul, on the other
hand, admitted he was a poor speaker and that some found
his preaching style contemptible (2 Cor. 10:10, 11:6). It's easy
to see how some Christians would have been so impressed
by the dynamic Apollos that they would have come to view
all other ministers, particularly Paul, as dull, ineffective, and
unworthy of being heard. And although Paul and Apollos
were colleagues and not adversaries (see 1 Cor. 3:6–9), some
overzealous followers held Apollos up as their guru, creating
friction in the Corinthian congregation (1:12).

   3. The Cephas party. We don't know for sure that Cephas—
Aramaic for Peter—ever visited Corinth. However, the Corinthian believers most likely knew that Jesus had renamed

him Peter, meaning "rock," and promised that the Church would be built upon him (Matt. 16:16–18; compare Eph. 2:19–20).[3] They probably also knew that Cephas was one of the pillars of the church, a missionary entrusted to the Jews (Gal. 2:7–9), and one of Jesus' original twelve disciples (Mark 3:16). With all these credentials, no wonder a personality cult, probably made up of Jewish Christians, was formed around him (1 Cor. 1:12).

4. **The Christ party.** Feeling they were too holy to be led by mere men, this group claimed to have received their teaching directly from the Lord. *They* were followers of Christ. They thought that since Christ is the head of the Church, human authorities were unnecessary. But instead of claiming that *they* belonged to *Christ,* they actually were claiming that *Christ* belonged to *them.* Even though they spoke pious words, their air of superiority was a stench to the nostrils of God. And so it is today.

> Their emphasis and their language are usually above reproach and their 'hot line' to God can be very intimidating. The net result of their presence in the church is that most others feel spiritually inadequate: 'We do not get clear messages from the Lord; we have no comparable sense of immediacy in prayer; we cannot match such unswerving certainty about the will of the Lord.' There is always a faint, but discernible, air of spiritual superiority when members of this group are present. It is not easy to cope with comments such as 'The Lord has told me that ...'.[4]

Where Is Your Focus?

Divisions lead to quarrels ... to cliques. But the root of it all is a misplaced focus.

You have five basic options for where to place your focus—each one clamors for the undivided attention of your eyes. One, you can fix your eyes on *things,*

---

3. Jesus' promise to Peter in Matthew 16:18 has been variously interpreted and hotly debated. Some sources that clearly discuss the interpretive options are these: "Matthew," by D. A. Carson, in *The Expositor's Bible Commentary* (Grand Rapids, Mich.: Zondervan Publishing House, 1984), vol. 8, pp. 366–69; *The Church in God's Program,* by Robert L. Saucy (Chicago, Ill.: Moody Press, 1972), pp. 62–64; *Difficult Passages in the Gospels,* by Robert H. Stein (Grand Rapids, Mich.: Baker Book House, 1984), pp. 86–88.

4. David Prior, *The Message of 1 Corinthians: Life in the Local Church* (Downers Grove, Ill.: InterVarsity Press, 1985), p. 34.

which leads to materialism and a nagging dissatisfaction. Two, you can focus on your *situation,* which teeters you between false security when your situation is good and devastation when things look bleak. Three, you can have your eyes on *yourself* ... become preoccupied, and suffer from ingrown eyeballitis. Four, you can focus on *others.* Here's where the Corinthians chose to turn their eyes. They bronzed people into idols, set them up as objects of worship. And five, the only right choice, you can gaze on the *Lord.*

> Fixing our eyes on Jesus, the author and
> perfecter of faith. (Heb. 12:2a)

Where's your focus? Is Christ the center of the picture, or is His image beginning to blur? Take time to refocus your life squarely on Him.

C. Their pride. The embers of the Corinthians' quarrels and cliques were fueled by combustible pride. They expressed their pride by boasting about who had baptized them (1 Cor. 1:13b). Apparently, they had come to believe that the authenticity of their faith rested on not only their baptism but also their baptizer. Paul challenges their boasting sharply:

> I thank God that I baptized none of you except Crispus
> and Gaius, that no man should say you were baptized
> in my name. (1 Cor. 1:14–15)

If the ceremony were as crucial as the Corinthians were making it out to be, Paul certainly would have been glad to perform it for everyone. But as he explains:

> For Christ did not send me to baptize, but to preach
> the gospel, not in cleverness of speech, that the cross
> of Christ should not be made void. (v. 17)

Paul emphasized the message of the cross, not baptism or oratory eloquence. Although he upheld these as important, he wanted to encourage the Corinthians to see that sharing the gospel was their major responsibility.[5]

III. Keeping the Family Together

Rising from the ashes of this congregation's smoldering relationships are three truths that will keep our churches out of divorce court.

---

5. A more complete discussion on baptism and its relationship to salvation can be found in the study guide *Growing Up in God's Family,* ed. Bill Watkins, from the Bible-teaching ministry of Charles R. Swindoll (Fullerton, Calif.: Insight for Living, 1986), pp. 15–16.

A. We divide our churches when we multiply quarrels, cliques, and pride. These only explode a church's bond, leaving members to cough and sputter in the smoky remains of a congregational divorce.

B. We subtract from the gospel when we add a display of the flesh. To emphasize individual personalities or preaching styles like the Corinthians did is to dim the light of the gospel. As members of God's family, we should seek to illumine the message of salvation and see that it infiltrates every dark corner of the world.

C. We exalt Christ when we lift up the cross and become obscure in its shadow. The love of Jesus flows best through a humble vessel that seeks to lift Him up without having to be noticed.

"That They May All Be One"

In the priestly prayer of Jesus—some of His last words to the Father before His death—the Savior bares His burden for believers.

"That they may all be one; even as Thou, Father, art in Me, and I in Thee, that they also may be in Us; that the world may believe that Thou didst send Me. And the glory which Thou hast given Me I have given to them; that they may be one, just as We are one; I in them, and Thou in Me, that they may be perfected in unity, that the world may know that Thou didst send Me, and didst love them, even as Thou didst love Me." (John 17:21–23)

As we have seen, the bond between members of a church can be easily torn or split. It may even be singed by sin's fires—fires such as quarrels, cliques, and pride.

To keep this from happening, or to mend the already frayed strands of unity, we need to focus on the One whose glory we share (John 17:22), leave our selfish desires in the ashes (Phil. 2:2–5), and cleave to our commitment to love one another (Col. 3:14).

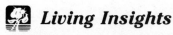 *Living Insights*

Study One ▬▬▬▬▬▬▬▬▬▬▬▬▬▬▬▬▬▬▬▬▬▬▬

Paul's strong rebuke to the Corinthian believers is well deserved. The divisiveness that swept the church was a sign of immaturity. Part of growing up is knowing what to major in and what to leave as a minor part of life. Let's clarify this idea.

- The text we covered concludes with the significance of the gospel. To emphasize its importance, Paul contrasts it with baptism. How important is it? Conduct your own Scripture search. Using New Testament passages that mention baptism—you might consult a concordance for help—jot down the biblical facts concerning this subject.

New Testament Teaching on Baptism	
Verses	Facts

Continued on next page

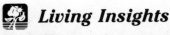 *Living Insights*

Study Two ━━━━━━━━━━━━━

The gospel is made void when it is preached with cleverness of speech (1 Cor. 1:17). This raises a very delicate issue—how does one balance the *simplicity* of the gospel with its *excellence?* How do you outstandingly present the truth without drawing attention to yourself? What keeps excellent qualities from becoming slick qualities?

• Is it wrong, as a Christian, to be committed to excellence? How do you achieve balance on this issue in your life? Write down your thoughts in the space provided below.

Simplicity and Excellence: A Balance

_____

_____

_____

_____

_____

_____

_____

_____

_____

_____

_____

Human Intellect versus Divine Wisdom

1 Corinthians 1:18–25

In the beginning God created man in His own image. The competition began when man insisted on returning the compliment.

People have created every false conception of God imaginable. Not only have they worked to make their deities palatable to the human mind, but they have set up their intellects—and therefore themselves—as gods. One of Christianity's archenemies, atheist Ayn Rand, says,

> "And now I see the face of god, and I raise this god over the earth, this god whom men have sought since men came into being, this god who will grant them joy and peace and pride. "This god, this one word: I."[1]

Representing New Age thought, performer Shirley MacLaine also allies herself with the losing side:

> "We already know everything. The knowingness of our divinity is the highest intelligence. And to *be* what we already know is the free will. Free will is simply the enactment of the realization you are God, a realization that you are divine."[2]

The rules of Christianity are unintelligible to those on the man-centered team. For Christianity neither flatters human beings nor presents God in an easily palatable form. But as C. S. Lewis remarks,

> That is one of the reasons I believe Christianity. It is a religion you could not have guessed. If it offered us just the kind of universe we had always expected, I should feel we were making it up. But, in fact, it is not the sort of thing anyone would have made up. It has just that queer twist about it that real things have.[3]

In 1 Corinthians, we find the believers at Corinth playing for the wrong side. So Paul opens God's playbook and explains His truth as something they would never expect or invent: a crucified Messiah and a crucified self as the way to life everlasting.

---

1. Ayn Rand, *For the New Intellectual* (New York, N.Y.: New American Library, 1961), p. 65.

2. As quoted by Douglas R. Groothuis in *Unmasking the New Age* (Downers Grove, Ill.: Inter-Varsity Press, 1986), p. 26.

3. C. S. Lewis, *Mere Christianity,* rev. and enl. (New York, N.Y.: Macmillan Publishing Co., 1952), pp. 47–48.

I. A Few Reminders about the Corinthians

The Corinthian Christians were an arrogant lot. They tucked their thumbs under their suspenders and bragged about incidental things like who baptized them (1 Cor. 1:12–15). Their pride led them to elevate human speech and thought over the good news about Jesus' death. In short, the gospel's heart was being trampled by the feet of humanism. This pseudointellectualism had to be stopped and replaced with the wisdom of God. They needed to come face-to-face with the meaning of the cross.

II. The Message of the Cross—Selfless Living

Christ's death is central to salvation—a process that begins with justification, advances by sanctification, and climaxes in glorification. Here Paul speaks directly to the second phase—progressive sanctification, where we are delivered from sin's power through the life of cross-bearing.

> For the word of the cross is to those who are perishing foolishness, but to us who are *being saved* it is the power of God. (v. 18, emphasis added)

The words *being saved*[4] indicate a process . . . a daily death to self.

A Word about Dying to Self

Dying to self does not require a morbid, introspective inferiority complex that leads to insecurity. Actually, those who have truly died to themselves depend solely on God . . . they no longer have to rely on their own plans and intellect to see them through. They are the most secure people on earth (see 2 Cor. 12:10).

In Luke 9:22–24, Jesus tells us what it means to die to self.

> "The Son of Man must suffer many things, and be rejected by the elders and chief priests and scribes, and be killed, and be raised up on the third day. . . . If anyone wishes to come after Me, let him deny himself, and take up his cross daily, and follow Me. For whoever wishes to save his life shall lose it, but whoever loses his life for My sake, he is the one who will save it."

In the same way that Jesus had to die and be raised, so we, too, must die to ourselves in order to be raised to everlasting life.

---

4. Or "that are in the way of salvation." Robert Jamieson, A. R. Fausset, and David Brown, *A Commentary, Critical, Experimental, and Practical, on the Old and New Testaments* (n.d.; reprint, Grand Rapids, Mich.: William B. Eerdmans Publishing Co., 1984), vol. 3, p. 285. Known by Greek scholars as an *iterative present tense,* "being saved" does not mean a continuing flow like a running engine but indicates an action much like chewing. In the same way that we eat a meal one bite at a time, we *experience* the cross's message in bite-size pieces.

III. The Human Intellect—Rival of Cross-Bearing

For unbelievers the message of death to self seems either incomprehensible, moronic, or absurd. It doesn't make sense to them, so they won't accept it. But, using the Lord's words, Paul reminds us: "For it is written, 'I will destroy the wisdom of the wise, / And the cleverness of the clever I will set aside' " (1 Cor. 1:19b).

A. An Old Testament example. The passage Paul quotes in verse 19 comes from Isaiah 29:14b. Isaiah made this prophecy when Israel had long been divided into two nations through civil war (1 Kings 12). The northern half called itself Israel, while the southern half was called Judah. The context of verse 14b concerns the Israelites' prideful actions, which brought down an edict from God. The ferocious Assyrian army was poised on Israel's border like a tiger ready to pounce. Instead of turning to God for protection, Israel followed human counsel and formed an alliance with Egypt (2 Kings 17:4). Relying on human force, human wisdom, and human power, she compromised her standard of separation from pagan nations . . . and the results were tragic. Israel was looking for wisdom in the intellect of man, but the scoreboard revealed that she came up short. She played on the wrong side and lost (see 2 Kings 17).[6]

---

5. See Michael P. Green's "The Meaning of Cross-Bearing," in *Bibliotheca Sacra* 140 (April–June 1983), pp. 124–27.

6. Contrast this with Judah's righteous King Hezekiah. When war-hungry Assyria had swallowed Israel and turned to devour Judah, Hezekiah humbled himself before God (2 Kings 19:1) and trusted Him to deliver the nation—which God did with a frightening display of His supernatural power (vv. 32–37; see also 2 Chron. 32:1–23, Isa. 36–37).

B. New Testament examples. Pointing his long, bony finger,
Paul now searches the congregation of Corinth.

> Where is the wise man? Where is the scribe? Where
> is the debater of this age? (1 Cor. 1:20a)

The wise man was the unsaved Gentile intellectual. The scribe,
the Jewish intellectual. And the debater, the Greek philosopher.
The implication of Paul's rhetorical question is "Nowhere; for
God 'brings them to nought.' "[7] With human thought as their
god, these members of the intellectual team delighted in probing
questions, yet they found no answers. They were looking in the
wrong playbook.

C. Contemporary examples. Even in our day, "the world
through its wisdom [has] not come to know God" (v. 21a). Bril-
liant astronomers chart the orbits and shapes of the planets.
But their telescopes never lead them to God. Astronauts, some
of the finest specimens of humanity, explore other planets. But
they don't discover God. Scientists peer through their micro-
scopes and record the details of a world invisible to human
eyes—scrutinizing, analyzing, hypothesizing, theorizing. But
their spiritual lenses are also microscopic, so they never see
God. Intellectual educators read and study and probe the clas-
sics. But in all their humanistic research, they, too, never find
God. No, "the world through its wisdom [has] not come to know
God."

IV. The Cross—The Way to Salvation

So what does it take to find God? Paul answers this question in
verse 21b: "God was well-pleased through the foolishness of the
message preached to save those who believe." Here Paul acknowledges the message of the cross as foolishness—not from God's
point of view, but from man's. He amplifies his point in verse 22:
"For indeed Jews ask for signs, and Greeks search for widsom." The

---

7. Jamieson, Fausset, and Brown, *A Commentary on the Old and New Testaments,* p. 285.

expectations of the Jews and Greeks would not allow them to accept the "foolishness" of the gospel message.

A. The Jews' response. The "Jews ask for signs" to verify the gospel. They demand a victorious Messiah, heralded by miracles, who will conquer their enemies and restore the glories of David's kingdom (Matt. 27:42; Mark 8:11; Luke 1:68–75, 24:21; Acts 1:6).[8] Instead, the Jews are presented with a man who refused to give them the signs they sought (Matt. 12:38–41) and, while claiming to be their king, wound up naked on a cross, laid in a borrowed tomb (see Matt. 27). No white horse. No shining lance. How could the Jews believe that this Jesus was their long-awaited Savior (1 Cor. 1:23)?

B. The Greeks' response. The Greeks, on the other hand, "search for wisdom." They look for a proud philosopher-king who will satisfy their intellectual curiosity (Acts 17:18–21). Instead, they are told about a divine ruler who humbles Himself to be born a Jew, grows into manhood virtually unrecognized, and spends three years speaking mysterious parables and healing all kinds of illnesses. He ends his brief ministry betrayed by His own people and executed by crucifixion—the most despised form of capital punishment used by the Roman Empire.[9] This whole matter scandalized the Greek mind-set (1 Cor. 1:23).

C. Paul's power play. In verses 23–25, Paul makes a strong case for playing on the right side.

> But we preach Christ crucified, to Jews a stumbling block, and to Gentiles foolishness, but to those who are the called, both Jews and Greeks, Christ the power of God and the wisdom of God. Because the foolishness of God is wiser than men, and the weakness of God is stronger than men.

The Crucified Christ and You

What do you think of the cross? Do you trust that Jesus' death and Resurrection—what appear to be foolishness—are the very power and wisdom of God? Or do you stand with arms folded across your chest, skeptical—

---

8. See S. G. F. Brandon's *Jesus and the Zealots* (New York, N.Y.: Charles Scribner's Sons, 1967).

9. The Roman citizen's attitude toward crucifixion was expressed well by Cicero: " 'Even if we are threatened with death, we may die free men. But the executioner, the veiling of the head, and the very word "cross" should be far removed not only from the person of a Roman citizen but from his thoughts, his eyes, and ears. For it is not only the actual occurrence of these things or the endurance of them, but liability to them, the expectation, nay, the mere mention of them, that is unworthy of a Roman citizen and a free man.' " As quoted by Green in "The Meaning of Cross-Bearing," p. 132, fn. 48.

demanding a convincing sign, an irrefutable argument, before you'll consider turning to the cross for salvation? Remember: His foolishness is wiser than our wisdom; and His weakness, stronger than our strength. So lay down your pride, take up your cross . . . and be saved.

V. Two Questions for Us

The Corinthians were clothing the cross in the rags of human intellect. Yet Paul knew that if they failed to cling to the unadulterated wisdom of God found in the crucified Christ, they would never experience the abundant life that Jesus promised. The cross of Christ and our personal crosses are inseparable. But putting this all together is sometimes difficult. Let's answer two questions raised by this lesson.

A. **Must we toss aside our intellect before accepting the gospel of crucifixion?** We may need to abandon some of our expectations, demands, and rationalizations, but we never have to violate sound reason in order to believe.[10] We must, however, surrender our wills to the Savior and allow His Spirit to transform our minds so we can become fully aligned with God (Rom. 12:1–2).

B. **How do we die to our sinful selves?** By daily turning our backs on our self-centered wills and kneeling before the crucified Messiah, harmonizing our every thought, word, and deed with His will. And since God is life (1 John 1:1; 5:11, 20), what have we really got to lose?

---

10. See Frederic R. Howe's *Challenge and Response: A Handbook of Christian Apologetics* (Grand Rapids, Mich.: Zondervan Publishing House, 1982).

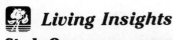 *Living Insights*

Who is the most intelligent person you can think of? Einstein? Curie? da Vinci? Shakespeare? Dickinson? Plato? Mozart? In comparison to the great wisdom of God, their combined geniuses wouldn't fill an atom. Yet, in the non-Christian world, God's wisdom is thought of as foolishness. The concluding words of 1 Corinthians 1 have much to say on this subject.

• One way of digging deeper into a passage of Scripture is to paraphrase—write out the text in your own words. Let's try this on 1 Corinthians 1:18–25. Paraphrasing will allow you to amplify the meanings and emotions within the text.

1 Corinthians 1:18–25

_____

_____

_____

_____

_____

_____

_____

_____

_____

_____

_____

_____

_____

_____

_____

_____

_____

Continued on next page

Study Two ▬▬▬▬▬▬▬▬▬▬▬▬▬▬▬▬▬▬▬▬▬▬▬▬▬▬▬▬▬▬▬▬▬

The gospel is foolishness to those without it. Yet, when Christ enters their lives, people change. Do you remember the stumbling blocks that kept you from believing in Christ? How did you overcome them? What did you consider to be foolish about the gospel message?

● Keeping in mind those stumbling blocks, use the following chart to write down some that bothered you the most. Then write down some ways to make those stumbling blocks into stepping-stones. In other words, how can God's wisdom shine forth so that people can discover His true character?

The "Foolishness" of God	
Stumbling Blocks	Stepping-stones

Profound Simplicity

1 Corinthians 1:26–2:5

Junk art. Juxtaposed, these words seem contradictory—like opposite poles of a magnet, repelling each other more violently the closer they're pushed together. Indeed, some junk art looks like the tortured remains of a high-speed two-car collision. But other works display grace, precision, beauty, and humor.

On a wall hangs a painting of a well-kept country road lined with pecan trees and yellow wildflowers. Attached to the canvas is a Model T made from discards—old thimbles, piano strings, rusted clock gears, bent paper clips, scratched door hinges, and cabinet knobs. Each part is virtually worthless. But the hands of a craftsman have turned the useless odds and ends into an extraordinary piece of art.

Apart from Christ, we are spiritual junk—good for practically nothing except littering His creation. But when we let Him take over our lives, He goes to work like a master artisan, straightening our twisted wills, sanding our coarse-grained characters, and mending our broken hearts. At first our transformation is hardly noticeable. But in time, His artistry begins to glisten. People look and admire, some perplexed about how the change took place . . . others clearly seeing the handiwork of God. As much as we might want to take credit for our makeover, deep within we know that the Lord deserves all the recognition. *He* has made us useful and attractive. *He* has molded our worthless lives into priceless works of art.

But sometimes we forget our junkyard beginnings. Our pride stands erect and parades our spiritual charms. We act as if God performed great work on us because we gave Him high-quality material to shape. In other words, we behave just as the Corinthian Christians did.

In 1 Corinthians 1:26–2:5, Paul sets the record straight. He reminds us that were it not for God's gracious intervention in our lives, we would still be rubbish.

I. Called from the Dump

Without God, all human beings—from the crème de la crème to the broken and wounded on skid row—are rotting away in the dump of sin. Despite our filthy condition, God mercifully reaches down, plucks us from the garbage heap, and transforms us into valuable art.

A. The facts. Paul starts this part of his rebuke by giving the Corinthians the hard facts about their call.

> For consider your calling, brethren, that there were not many wise according to the flesh, not many mighty, not many noble. (v. 26)

33

With few exceptions, these believers were on the bottom rung of the social ladder. Their ranks were full of fornicators, adulterers, effeminates, homosexuals, idolaters, thieves, coveters, drunkards, revilers, and swindlers (6:9–10). They were nothing but door hinges, thumbtacks, and thimbles. Even so, God stooped to pick them up and put them into His frame. Because, as Paul tells them in chapter 6, they

> were washed, ... sanctified, ... justified in the name
> of the Lord Jesus Christ, and in the Spirit of our God.
> (v. 11)

"God Has Chosen"

Out of His grace, God stoops and saves the nobodies, the nothings, the junk. He has chosen the *foolish* things, the *weak* things, the *base,* the *despised,* and "*the things that are not*" (1:27–28, emphasis added). Things scarcely worth mentioning, things littering the ground, God has been pleased to pick up and enfold in His arms.

Such grace should remind us that the artist, not the art, should get the honor. Why has He bothered to make any of us valuable? As Paul tells the Corinthians, "that no man should boast before God" (v. 29).[1] God will not tolerate the proud. So He steps on their egos by lifting up the dregs of society as honored citizens of His kingdom. By debasing the arrogant, He humbles them, makes them see their impoverishment, and enables them to receive His great riches. The Lord accepts them no other way (compare Dan. 4:28–37).

Leaving Pride in the Trash Bin

Pride is self-deification. It is that competitive drive within us to be richer, cleverer, better-looking, or more powerful than someone else. We like the feeling and recognition that comes from standing above the rest. And we seek these pleasures in everything we do—including our pursuit of God.

> No sooner do we believe that God loves us than
> there is an impulse to believe that He does so,
> not because He is Love, but because we are

---

1. Verse 31 appears to contradict verse 29. But one small difference—a difference in prepositions—indicates a radical difference in mind-sets. "That no man should boast *before* God" (v. 29, emphasis added) means we are not to challenge Him as the artist of our lives. But we are told to "boast *in* the Lord" (v. 31, emphasis added). We are to boast in His transforming power, in His authority, in His grace.

intrinsically lovable. The Pagans obeyed this impulse unabashed; a good man was "dear to the gods" because he was good. We, being better taught, resort to subterfuge. Far be it from us to think that we have virtues for which God could love us. But then, how magnificently we have repented! As Bunyan says, describing his first and illusory conversion, "I thought there was no man in England that pleased God better than I." Beaten out of this, we next offer our own humility to God's admiration. Surely He'll like *that?* Or if not that, our clear-sighted and humble recognition that we still lack humility. Thus, depth beneath depth and subtlety within subtlety, there remains some lingering idea of our own, our very own, attractiveness.[2]

Have you abandoned your pride, tossed it in the wastebasket, and left it behind? Or do you keep picking it out from the rest of the trash to polish and display?

B. The contrast. Next, Paul contrasts the Corinthians' ordinary characteristics with the beauty of Jesus.

> But by His doing you are in Christ Jesus, who became to us wisdom from God, and righteousness and sanctification, and redemption. (1 Cor. 1:30)

The world looks for heroes; God seeks the humble. The world is impressed by power, prestige, and money; God is impressed only by Christ—the gentlest, most humble person who ever walked the earth. Therefore, God has given His Son preeminence over all creation and made Him our wisdom. Christ is our righteousness; through Him we are justified, released from the penalty of sin (Rom. 3:21–26). He is our sanctification; through Him we are made holy, liberated daily from sin's power (1 Thess. 4:7, 1 Pet. 1:1–2). He is also our redemption; through Him we are glorified and freed forever from sin's presence (Rom. 8:23, Rev. 21:9–22:5). Alone, we are nothing. But in Christ, we are invaluable. The difference lies in Him, not us. Thus, if we boast at all, we should boast in Him (1 Cor. 1:31). As the Lord told Jeremiah,

> "Let not a wise man boast of his wisdom, and let not the mighty man boast of his might, let not a rich man boast of his riches; but let him who boasts boast of this, that he understands and knows Me, that I am

2. C. S. Lewis, *The Four Loves* (New York, N.Y.: Harcourt Brace Jovanovich, 1960), p. 180.

the Lord who exercises lovingkindness, justice, and
righteousness on earth; for I delight in these things."
(Jer. 9:23–24)

II. Paul's Beautifying Ministry

The Corinthians' salvation proves that God chooses the ordinary
rather than the outstanding. Paul's ministry in Corinth lent further
support to this truth.

A. His message. Continuing his argument in chapter 2, Paul
admits his own ordinariness to the Corinthians.

> And when I came to you, brethren, I did not come
> with superiority of speech or of wisdom, proclaiming
> to you the testimony of God. (v. 1)

Although Paul was a deep thinker and a good debater (Acts
19:8–10, 26:24–29; 2 Pet. 3:15–16), he could not match the ora-
torical skills and commanding presence of an Apollos. But this
didn't matter to him, because his goal was to highlight one
message: "Jesus Christ, and Him crucified" (1 Cor. 2:2). Everything else was superfluous.

B. His method. When Paul served the Corinthians, he did so "in
weakness and in fear and in much trembling"[3] (v. 3). This forced
him to depend on the Lord perhaps more than he ever had
before (compare Phil. 2:12–13). The result was staggering. What
he lacked in courage and talent, God made up in power. As Paul
spoke, the gospel exploded throughout the streets of Corinth.
The Holy Spirit moved into shops, homes, temples, synagogues,
and alleys. People came and listened to unimpressive Paul, and
many walked away singing God's praises. Like Paul, we may not
be fearless souls or great public speakers, but then we don't
have to be. The Lord will reveal His strength through our weakness. All He asks is that we rely on Him as we carry out the
tasks He has for us.

C. His motive. Why didn't Paul take speech lessons from the
expert communicators of his day? Why didn't he try to throw
in some clever lines, entertaining jokes, or spellbinding argu-
ments to wow his audience? Because he wanted God's power,
not human wisdom, to convince the Corinthians to accept the
truth. Paul told them:

---

3. "Not cowardly *fear,* but *trembling anxiety to perform duty;* anxious conscientiousness in
contrast to 'eye service' [Eph. 6:5, 2 Cor. 7:15, Phil. 2:12]. His very weakness, as that of Christ
crucified, his theme, was made the power of God [1 Cor. 1:27]." From *A Commentary, Critical,
Experimental, and Practical, on the Old and New Testaments,* by Robert Jamieson, A. R.
Fausset, and David Brown (n.d.; reprint, Grand Rapids, Mich.: William B. Eerdmans Publishing
Co., 1984), vol. 3, p. 287.

And my message and my preaching were not in per-
suasive words of wisdom, but in demonstration of
the Spirit and of power, that your faith should not
rest on the wisdom of men, but on the power of God.
(1 Cor. 2:4–5)

Human ingenuity and rhetorical flourish will never bring people
to salvation. Only the simplicity of the gospel coupled with the
work of the Spirit can humble people and lead them to redemption.

III. Purging Pride from Our Frames

The Corinthian Christians had forgotten they were junk art. They
looked into their frames and took credit for the beauty and order
God had wrought. Lest we judge them too harshly, we must admit
to sometimes allowing our pride to draw us into the same sin. But
we needn't despair. Our arrogance can be squelched. Obeying the
following four directives will help.

A. Remember the pit. God is fashioning us into priceless works
of art, perfect images of His Son (Rom. 8:29, Phil. 3:20–21). But
let's never forget that He found us in the dump of human deprav-
ity—without purpose, significance, or hope.

B. Refuse the praise. If we were to take credit for what God
has done through us, we would be like sculptures accepting
applause for the sculptor's genius. This doesn't mean that when
people express appreciation for how we've benefited them we
should say, "You're welcome, but God gets all the glory—praise
the Lord!" Humility on parade is no better than a showy display
of our supposed superiority. Rather, we should offer a simple
thank-you, humbly recognizing that we are nothing without Him.

C. Recognize the artist. We are not remaking ourselves—God
is. He is following His design and using His tools. We are simply
the broken and bent materials He has graciously chosen to
transform.

D. Rest in God's power. Until we become like Christ, imperish-
able and immortal in soul and body (1 Cor. 15:42–44, 52–54),
we will be fragile. Circumstances will threaten to chip us . . .
crack us . . . even shatter us. But if we rely on God to empower
us, we will be able to handle any situation He permits to come
our way (1 Cor. 10:13).

Continued on next page

Living Insights

Through the ages, good communicators have been men and women committed to *clarity* and *simplicity*. This is the thrust of Paul's message in the passage we've just studied. Let's examine a few more biblical references on the value of simplicity and clarity.

● Take a few minutes to look up the verses below; then jot down your thoughts. Ask these questions: Why is clarity important? How does this verse describe simplicity?

Clarity and Simplicity

1 Corinthians 14:8–9 _____

_____

_____

2 Corinthians 3:12–18 _____

_____

_____

2 Corinthians 4:1–7 _____

_____

_____

Ephesians 4:14–15 _____

_____

_____

Colossians 4:6 _____

_____

_____

38

Living Insights

In 1 Corinthians 2:1–5, we observed Paul's message, method, and motive. What message are you most consistently giving? How would you describe your method of communication? Perhaps the most important question is this: What is your motive in communicating to other people? Use the space provided to answer these questions.

What message am I consistently communicating?

_____

_____

_____

_____

_____

What is my method of communication?

_____

_____

_____

_____

What is my motive in communicating with others?

_____

_____

_____

_____

_____

The Hidden Depths of God

1 Corinthians 2:6–16

The cold, black Antarctic.

A blocky, flat-topped iceberg crawls through the water. Colored brown, black, and green by a combination of sediment, plankton, and glacial blue ice, it measures about one hundred feet above sea level. What most people don't know, though, is that the biggest part of the iceberg lies beneath the freezing whitecaps—about six hundred feet under the surface.

God's wisdom is like the iceberg. To unbelievers, who see only the tip, it is intellectually treacherous, blindingly unrealistic, and desperately purposeless. But those who are graced by God's salvation see below the surface to the precious, quiet deeps.

Should it surprise us that unbelievers cannot see below the surface to the massive bulk of the excellence, truth, and wisdom of Christianity? This question is what concerns Paul in 1 Corinthians 2:6–16. In this lesson we will discover why unbelievers cannot plumb the depths of God's wisdom and how we, as believers, are able to understand the most hidden secrets of God.

I. Wisdom: The Main Idea

Paul has been telling the Corinthians that their "faith should not rest on the wisdom of men, but on the power of God" (2:5). But, realizing that some may interpret him to mean that Christianity is irrational, and that to believe in it is tantamount to committing intellectual suicide, he clears things up.

> Yet we do speak wisdom among those who are mature;
> a wisdom, however, not of this age, nor of the rulers of
> this age, who are passing away. (v. 6)

The wisdom spoken of here is *insight*—perception about people, problems, ourselves, life—known as "God's wisdom, . . . the thoughts of God, . . . the things of the Spirit, . . . the mind of Christ" (vv. 7, 11, 14, 16). And only the mature in Christ can possess this wisdom, which should give spiritual babes the incentive to grow. For the deeper we swim into Christian maturity, the more wisdom we'll have to live for the Lord (Heb. 5:14–6:1).

II. Wisdom and the Non-Christian

Paul gives three reasons why nonbelievers can see only the tip of the iceberg.

A. It's a mystery. Paul explains that believers "speak God's wisdom in a mystery" (1 Cor. 2:7a). The Greek word for *mystery* is *mustērion,* which conveys the idea of "secret" more than "mystery." A mystery is something that is complex, intertwined, hard

40

to grasp. But a secret is something that is clear to those who've been informed, while murky to those who haven't. To unbelievers, God's wisdom is a secret they aren't in on; when they listen to believers speaking its language, they hear only unintelligible whispers.

B. It's not understood. Paul goes on to describe God's wisdom as "the wisdom which none of the rulers of this age has understood" (v. 8a). The Greek word he uses for *understand* is *ginōskō,* which refers to a knowledge born of deep personal understanding.[1] Spiritual depth perception comes from experiential knowledge of God, not just intellectual comprehension of truths about Him. Reminding us about the human rulers who executed Jesus, Paul tells us that "if they had understood it, they would not have crucified the Lord of glory" (v. 8b). Had the human authorities understood who Jesus was, they would never have put the nails in His hands and feet.

Taking the Plunge

Unbelieving Bible scholars are like lazy scientists—those who might spend years just observing iceberg tips through high-powered lenses but never look below the surface to see what icebergs are really made of.

Are you tired of having a shallow understanding of God, His wisdom, His ways? Are you ready to plunge into a deeper knowledge of Him? If so, put on your wet suit, dive in, and experience the depths of His wisdom (Prov. 8:17, Matt. 7:7).

C. It's not learned. Last, Paul says that unbelievers cannot gain this insight through mere observation or experience:

"Things which eye has not seen and ear has not heard,
And which have not entered the heart of man,
All that God has prepared for those who love Him."
(1 Cor. 2:9)[2]

They can spend the next twenty years studying in the most prestigious schools, adding little letters to the ends of their

---

1. See Donald W. Burdick's "*Oida* and *Ginōskō* in the Pauline Epistles" in *New Dimensions in New Testament Study,* ed. Richard Longenecker and Merrill C. Tenney (Grand Rapids, Mich.: Zondervan Publishing House, 1974), pp. 344–56.

2. Taken from Isaiah 64:4, these words were addressed to the adversaries of God, to those who had claimed they were superior to Him. Therefore, the "eye," "ear," and "heart" mentioned in 1 Corinthians 2:9 refer to the unbeliever. As believers, we are not shut out from "all that God has prepared" for us.

names . . . being widely traveled and well-read, but they can never learn the depths God has for them. His wisdom can't be acquired empirically. It must be secured by the heart through faith.

III. Wisdom and the Christian

Paul now shares with the Corinthian believers how they, and we as modern-day saints, can discover the hidden treasures of God's wisdom.

A. The priority. God chooses those who trust in Him to be the recipients of His wisdom, as Paul explains in verse 10: "For *to us* God revealed them" (emphasis added). God reveals His wisdom to believers, not to the unbelieving intelligentsia, influential, or wealthy (1:27–30). We are God's priority based solely on His grace.

B. The process. Paul goes on to describe God's tool for revealing His wisdom.

> For to us God revealed them *through the Spirit;* for the Spirit searches all things, even the depths of God. For who among men knows the thoughts of a man except the spirit of the man, which is in him? Even so the thoughts of God no one knows except the Spirit of God. (vv. 10–11, emphasis added)

William Barclay, in his commentary on Paul's letters to the Corinthians, explains the significance of the Spirit's relationship to God and His role in edifying the believer.

> Paul lays down that the only person who can tell us about God is the Spirit of God. He uses a human analogy. There are feelings which are so personal, things which are so private, experiences which are so intimate that no one knows them except a man's own spirit. Paul argues that the same is true of God. There are deep and intimate things in him which only his Spirit knows; and that Spirit is the only person who can lead us into really intimate knowledge of God.[3]

The moment we place our faith in the Lord, the Holy Spirit joins our lives and begins transforming us into Christ's image (3:18). He indwells us (Rom. 8:9, 11), liberates us from the oppressive power of sin (vv. 1–17), "searches . . . the depths of God" (1 Cor. 2:10b), and communicates His thoughts to us as we draw upon His resources (vv. 11–12, John 16:13–15, Eph. 3:14–19).

C. The purpose. God promises to give us the Spirit the moment we are saved. No need to wait to receive Him—if we've trusted

3. William Barclay, *The Letters to the Corinthians,* rev. ed., The Daily Study Bible Series (Philadelphia, Pa.: Westminster Press, 1975), pp. 27–28.

in Jesus, the Spirit already lives within us. Paul tells why God does this for us.

> Now we have received, not the spirit of the world, but the Spirit who is from God, *that we might know the things freely given to us by God,* which things we also speak, not in words taught by human wisdom, but in those taught by the Spirit, combining spiritual thoughts with spiritual words. (1 Cor. 2:12–13, emphasis added)

Paul explains that the Spirit communicates the divine wisdom of Christianity because man could otherwise never understand it. " 'For sound wisdom has two sides' " (Job 11:6)—a surface and a depth. The Spirit is given to us that we might know the depth (1 Cor. 2:12b).

A Two-Sided Wisdom

One side of wisdom—the surface side—could be called the ministry of the Word. We often understand the Word when it has been preached because it has been explained in a way that ministers to our minds. But God wants more from us. He wants us to experience the other side of wisdom—the deep side—which we could call the ministry of the Spirit. This is where God's Spirit takes the ministry of the Word and plumbs it down under the surface currents to where He can minister to our hearts and souls.

IV. A Wrap-Up on Wisdom

In the last three verses of 1 Corinthians 2, Paul summarizes the main difference between unbelievers and believers.

A. The non-Christian. "A natural man," states Paul, "does not accept the things of the Spirit" for to him they are foolishness (v. 14a; compare 1:18, 21, 23). The natural man cannot understand them. Without the Holy Spirit's indwelling ministry, unbelievers will never experientially know the riches of the Spirit, for spiritual matters are "spiritually appraised" (2:14b). Unbelievers may grasp them superficially, but they will never know them personally and deeply.

B. The maturing Christian. The flip side of the unsaved person is the maturing Christian.

> But he who is spiritual appraises all things, yet he himself is appraised by no man. For who has known the mind of the Lord, that he should instruct Him? *But we have the mind of Christ.* (vv. 15–16, emphasis added)

43

Maturing Christians are those who have given the Spirit control of their lives. They still wrestle with sin, but they confess it daily, keeping their hearts constantly clean.

A Word to the Carnal

Being a believer doesn't necessarily mean that you have discovered the hidden depths of God's wisdom. Even though they are available for all believers, some choose to tread the shallow waters, eyes fixed only on the tip of the iceberg.

If you've entered the waters of Christianity but haven't yet given the Spirit control of your understanding, do so today. Let Him take you to the very depths of God.

 Living Insights

Study One ▬▬▬▬▬▬▬▬▬▬▬▬▬▬▬

In this beautifully written passage, we see how the "foolishness" of the gospel isn't foolish at all. Nor is it shallow. As the lesson title points out, these verses share with us the hidden depths of God.

- First Corinthians 2:6–16 teaches us that there is a vast wealth of wisdom unavailable to anyone—*except the Christian!* Reread this passage in your own Bible. Afterwards, read it from another version. Many times we discover new facets of God's Word when we read it in a different translation or paraphrase. Don't hurry. Spend some time lingering over the hidden depths of God.

 Living Insights

Study Two ▬▬▬▬▬▬▬▬▬▬▬▬▬▬▬

After studying the hidden depths of God, we should respond to the Lord with praise and thanksgiving for who He is. We should also thank Him for making the hidden things available to us through His Son, Jesus Christ. God has revealed much to us through His Spirit. The world cannot understand it. But it's ours, and we ought to give thanks for it.

- Let's use our Living Insights time to worship the Lord. Focusing on praise and thanksgiving, pray to Him verbally or write out your thoughts to Him in the space provided. Praise Him for who He is and what He has done for you. Thank Him for His gracious involvement in your life. Where would you be if He hadn't made Himself available to you? That thought alone should fuel your fires of prayer for quite some time.

Praise Him . . . Thank Him!

_____

_____
_____
_____
_____
_____

_____
_____
_____
_____

_____
_____
_____
_____

_____
_____
_____
_____

_____
_____
_____
_____

_____
_____
_____

The Pigpen Christian

1 Corinthians 2:14–3:4, Luke 15:11–32

Like modern-day Enochs, some Christians walk so closely to God that they live "heavenly" lives on earth.[1] It's not that all they ever have are golden-street, pearly-gate experiences. In fact, they often suffer deeply. But they carry with them the peace, faith, and steadfastness that only come to those who daily practice living in God's kingdom. These believers are on earth, but their hearts beat to the pulse of heaven.

Other Christians, heirs of the same kingdom, choose instead to live in the pigpen. Wallowing in sin's slop, they squander that part of their spiritual inheritance which is intended to be enjoyed on earth. They trade it for a romp in the slime of their selfishness. These earthly believers are still headed for heaven . . . but living like hell.

What about these pigpen Christians? What about these believers who continue to sin? One common theory is that they never were saved . . . that they believed in their heads but not in their hearts . . . that they never really "committed" themselves.[2] Another idea is that they *were* saved, but somehow lost their salvation. They sincerely found redemption, but let it slip through their muddy fingers.

Although some Scripture seems to support this last viewpoint, the answer Paul gives in 1 Corinthians best supports the Bible's truths about the eternal destiny of the pigpen Christian. In this lesson we will study Paul's rebuke to the carnal Corinthian believers and be challenged to come out of the pigpen of our own lives.

I. Three Kinds of People

In 1 Corinthians 2:14–3:4, Paul talks about three types of people—the natural, the spiritual, and the fleshly. As we'll see, the first group is made up of unbelievers; the other two, of Christians at different levels of spiritual maturity.

A. Natural people. These people are the lost, the unsaved, the spiritually dead. Paul describes them in 2:14:

> But a natural man does not accept the things of the Spirit of God; for they are foolishness to him, and he cannot understand them, because they are spiritually appraised.

---

1. "By faith Enoch was taken up so that he should not see death; . . . for he obtained the witness that before his being taken up he was pleasing to God" (Heb. 11:5; see also Gen. 5:21–24).

2. The Bible acknowledges this position (Matt. 7:21–23; Mark 4:16–17; 1 John 2:18–19; Jude 4, 12–13).

Natural people have pulled in the welcome mat from the door of their hearts, locked the dead bolt, and turned a deaf ear to Jesus' knocking (Rev. 3:20).

B. Spiritual people. These people are saved and are enjoying vital fellowship with God. They are active, productive members of His family. They "have the mind of Christ" (1 Cor. 2:16b)—a spiritual insight that natural people cannot have.

C. Fleshly people. The third group of people Paul talks about are the fleshly—believers rooting in the pigpens of their old natures, rebelling against the control of the Holy Spirit. This group filled the pews in the Corinthian church. Paul describes these carnal believers in four ways.

1. **They are Christians.** Paul addresses them as "saints" (1:2) and "brethren" (3:1a)—brothers and sisters in the Lord. Clearly, then, Paul is speaking to believers. Not mature believers, but "babes in Christ" (v. 1b; see also Heb. 5:12–14).

2. **They lack spiritual growth.** Paul tells the Corinthians:

   > I gave you milk to drink, not solid food; for you were not yet able to receive it. Indeed, even now you are not yet able. (1 Cor. 3:2)

   Nobody expects an infant to be able to eat a T-bone steak. Nor does anyone expect a new believer to be able to digest the meatier doctrines of the faith. New Christians need to be bottle-fed theology's basic formulas until they cut enough teeth to handle solid food (1 Pet. 2:2). The tragedy is that these Christians should have been mature, but were still babes in Christ; they should have been weaned, but were still clinging to their bottles (1 Cor. 3:2b).[3]

3. **They nurse unconfessed sin.** Carnal Christians feed their old natures and starve their new ones (v. 3; compare Rom. 6:6, 12–13; Eph. 4:17–24; Col. 3:1–10). In verse 3, Paul expresses his heartache over their spiritual emaciation: "For since there is jealousy and strife among you, are you not fleshly?"

4. **They resemble non-Christians.** Paul continues, "Are you not walking like mere men?" (v. 3b). Like pigs whose pure pink flesh is hidden beneath layers of squalid muck, carnal Christians mask their redemption with the mud of the world. It's as though they were never washed by the Savior's blood.

---

3. The word *flesh* in verse 1 means "weak, little, in the flesh"—a condition one can't help being in. But notice Paul's word choice in verse 3. He calls the Corinthians *fleshly,* meaning "characterized by flesh, governed by flesh—a willful condition." The difference between these two words describes the Corinthians. They were spiritually immature, and they had no excuse.

> ## Savior or Lord?
>
> People are able to understand the lordship of Christ only after accepting Jesus as Savior and letting the Spirit teach them God's truth.
>
> There are two sides to His relationship with us. As our Savior, He gives us a positional relationship that is unshakable: we are guaranteed salvation from eternal punishment (Rom. 8:1).[4] And as our Lord, He gives us an experiential relationship—one that can be broken and scarred by sin and healed only by confession (1 John 1:9). Without confession, the Lord has only one choice—divine discipline.
>
> Are you still in the high chair only gumming the Word? If so, it's time to start cutting your spiritual teeth so you can chew the solid meat of God's truth. Confess that sin, and accept Jesus not only as Savior, but also as Lord.

II. A Tale of Two Prodigals

In Luke 15:11–32, Jesus tells us about a man with two sons—treasured members of his family, but rebels who wandered from their father's love. Commonly known as the story of the prodigal son, this tale actually talks about two prodigal sons. Only one son actually ran away and wound up in a pigpen, but the other son, who stayed home and acted respectably, was in a pigpen too—rolling and squealing in the mire of his self-righteousness.[5]

A. **The runaway rebel.** The younger son cameos one type of carnal Christian, the type who doesn't try to mask his rebellion with a false loyalty. This famous short story opens with him demanding his share of the inheritance and the father granting his request.

1. **The downfall.** Once the son had the money in his hot little hands, he "gathered everything together and went on a journey into a distant country, and there he squandered his estate with loose living" (v. 13b).

---

4. Some helpful discussions on the believer's eternal security are given in *Once Saved, Always Saved,* by R. T. Kendall (Chicago, Ill.: Moody Press, 1983) and the study guide *Growing Up in God's Family,* ed. Bill Watkins, from the Bible-teaching ministry of Charles R. Swindoll (Fullerton, Calif.: Insight for Living, 1986), p. 57.

5. For fascinating exegetical and historical observations on this parable, see *Poet and Peasant AND Through Peasant Eyes,* combined edition, by Kenneth E. Bailey (Grand Rapids, Mich.: William B. Eerdmans Publishing Co., 1983), pp. 158–206.

Soon, this son reached his desperation level.

> "Now when he had spent everything, a severe famine occurred in that country, and he began to be in need. And he went and attached himself to one of the citizens of that country, and he sent him into his fields to feed swine. And he was longing to fill his stomach with the pods that the swine were eating, and no one was giving anything to him." (Luke 15:14–16)

2. The restoration. Knee-deep in swine slop, hungry, alone, he finally comes to his senses and makes plans to go home to his father (vv. 17–18), rehearsing this little softening-up speech:

> " ' "Father, I have sinned against heaven, and in your sight; I am no longer worthy to be called your son; make me as one of your hired men." ' "
> (vv. 18b–19)

The story then shifts to his father, who, having longed for his son's return, sees him " 'while he was still a long way off' " (v. 20a). Far from rebuking his prodigal son, the father feels compassion for him, running to embrace and kiss him (v. 20b). The son begins his rehearsed speech (v. 21), but instead of listening to him, the father sends his slaves to get his best robe, a ring, and sandals to put on him.[6] Then he commands his slaves to prepare for a celebration (v. 23). For, he exclaims, " ' "this son of mine was dead, and has come to life again; he was lost, and has been found" ' " (v. 24).

---

6. The robe was a sign of acceptance; the ring, a sign of authority and trust; and the sandals, the sign of a free man. Paul N. Benware, *Luke, the Gospel of the Son of Man* (Chicago, Ill.: Moody Press, 1985), p. 107.

B. The respectable rebel. The older son didn't share his father's joy over his brother's return. When he heard about it, he became angry and refused to join the festivities (v. 28). He complained to his father:

> " 'Look! For so many years I have been serving you,
> and I have never neglected a command of yours; and
> yet you have never given me a kid, that I might be
> merry with my friends; but when this son of yours
> came, who has devoured your wealth with harlots,
> you killed the fattened calf for him.' " (vv. 29–30)

Notice the pride in this rebel's words. He drags his brother's name back through the mud and denies any familial relationship with him. With another demonstration of sacrificial love, the father reaches out to his disgruntled son, appealing to him to rejoice over his brother's return.

> "And he said to him, 'My child, you have always been
> with me, and all that is mine is yours. But we had to
> be merry and rejoice, for this brother of yours was
> dead and has begun to live, and was lost and has
> been found.' " (vv. 31–32)

Jesus leaves the older son in the spiritual pigpen, never telling us whether or not he decided to clean up his attitude and join his brother's welcome-home party. Clearly, Jesus expects us to finish the story with our own response.

When you look in the mirror, if you see either of these two sons, remember that the Father wants a relationship with you. He wants you home, and He wants you to love Him. You don't have to clean up your life; just come home by confessing your sins, and He will cleanse you (1 John 1:9). "A broken and a contrite heart, O God, Thou wilt not despise" (Ps. 51:17b).

 Living Insights

Study One ▬▬▬▬▬▬▬▬▬▬▬▬▬▬▬▬▬▬▬▬▬▬▬▬▬▬▬▬▬

Most of us tend to divide the human race into *two* groups—Christians and non-Christians. But this all-important passage in 1 Corinthians shows us there are really *three:* the natural, the spiritual, and the fleshly.

- Keep these three categories in mind while thinking through the lives of some memorable Bible characters. Using the following chart, write in the names of several who come to mind. What category does each individual fall into? For many of them, it depends on the particular period of their lives you are recalling. Just as we took a longer look at the story of the prodigal son, take some extra time to study one or two of the characters on your list.

The Three Types of People		
Natural	Spiritual	Fleshly

Continued on next page

Living Insights

What is a *spiritual* man? How is spirituality evidenced? In what ways does this apply to *your* life?

- Answer these questions in the space provided. Make sure your answers are biblical. Start with 1 Corinthians 2:14–3:4 and branch out from there. Be specific and practical.

How can I be a spiritual person?

_____

_____

_____

_____

_____

_____

_____

_____

_____

_____

_____

_____

_____

Three Pictures of You
1 Corinthians 3:5–17

Picture it. An unbeliever asks you to explain salvation, and you say: "Salvation is the act whereby God graciously delivers fallen human beings from the consequences of sin through the placement of their faith in His Son, Jesus Christ." Like reading Aristotle to a three-year-old, giving unbelievers this erudite definition would probably make them give up on the whole thing.

But if you told them: "Trust in Jesus, and He will pry open sin's claws and let you soar free," they would probably want to hear more. You will have spoken through their minds to their hearts, where salvation really happens.

Both definitions mean essentially the same thing. But the second one, full of word pictures, helps us see, feel, and desire deliverance. Vividness makes the difference.

When it came to communicating through images, Jesus was a master. He used them frequently and skillfully with His audiences to express deep and difficult truths. He spoke of Himself as a vine that nourishes its branches (John 15:1–5), a shepherd who lays down his life for his sheep (10:11), the one true light in a darkened world (8:12), the bread of life (6:35).

Paul follows in Jesus' rhetorical footsteps. While addressing the Corinthians' problems in 1 Corinthians 3:5–17, he uses three word pictures they would easily have grasped and that apply to us today. So, as we study this passage, let these familiar, concrete images challenge your heart.

I. Growing into a Healthy Plant
Following the teachers of the Word rather than the God of the Word, the Corinthians proved themselves saplings in the faith. Paul criticizes their immaturity:

> What then is Apollos? And what is Paul? Servants through whom you believed, even as the Lord gave opportunity to each one. (v. 5)

He goes on to make a clear distinction between the sowers and the soil.

A. The sowers. The sowers are those who plant, water, fertilize, prune, and harvest people for Jesus. Paul describes them as "*servants* through whom you believed" (v. 5b, emphasis added), not gods, which the Corinthians were making them out to be. He also shows them to be *partners;* "I planted, Apollos watered" (v. 6a)—working together, not competing to outgreen each other's thumbs. Paul explains that such competition would be inane, for

> neither the one who plants nor the one who waters
> is anything, but God who causes the growth. (v. 7b)

Where did their growth come from? God. Apollos and Paul were the sowers, but God alone caused the growth.

B. The soil. Whom has God chosen for His soil? Paul explains, "For we are God's fellow workers; you are God's field" (v. 9a). His goal is that we be His productive field—soil that produces blossoming, reproducing plants.

How Does Your Garden Grow?

Like the Corinthians, are you growing crab grass in your garden? Bitter weeds? Weeping willows?

Or are you a rose—blooming, fragrant, radiating encouragement to all who come near you?

Just as Paul urged the Corinthians, I urge you today to grow up—to transplant the refreshing fruit of the Spirit where the rotten fruit of pride grows (Gal. 5:22–23), and acknowledge God as the one who nurtures you to maturity.

> Every good thing bestowed and every perfect
> gift is from above, coming down from the Father
> of lights, with whom there is no variation, or
> shifting shadow. (James 1:17)

II. Building on a Solid Foundation

After using the plant image to emphasize the Corinthians' need for maturity, Paul depicts the Corinthian church as a building, stressing the quality they should strive for in constructing their spiritual structure. He takes them full circle through each stage—from laying the foundation, through the actual construction, to the final inspection. And in this image, he gives some of Christianity's nuts and bolts.

A. The foundation. Paul, the foreman of the job, begins by giving some of the basics of the Corinthian project. First, he tells how the architectural layout was drawn up—"according to the grace of God which was given to me, as a wise master builder" (1 Cor. 3:10a). Then he hones in on the foundation.

> For no man can lay a foundation other than the one
> which is laid, which is Jesus Christ.[1] (v. 11)

---

1. "The concept of Christ as the foundation . . . was strengthened in the early church by the use of [Isaiah 28:16] ('Behold, I am laying in Zion for a foundation a stone, a tested stone . . .')." From *1 and 2 Corinthians,* ed. F. F. Bruce (Greenwood, S.C.: Attic Press, 1971), p. 44.

B. The construction. After cementing the importance of the foundation in the Corinthians' minds, Paul gives them an on-the-job warning about their methods of construction.

> I laid a foundation, and another is building upon it.
> But let each man be careful *how* he builds upon it.
> (v. 10b, emphasis added)

Notice that Paul's focus is on the quality of the building. Because of the excellence of the foundation, he urges them to use only the best materials—long-lasting ones, like gold, silver, and precious stones, rather than the temporal and flammable ones of wood, hay, and straw (v. 12).

C. The inspection. Paul explains why it's so important to maintain high quality control on the building materials: because every believer's work will be inspected. At the judgment seat of Christ, God will reward believers for their work (see 2 Cor. 5:10). As Paul says:

> If any man's work which he has built upon it remains,
> he shall receive a reward. If any man's work is burned
> up, he shall suffer loss; but he himself shall be saved,
> yet so as through fire. (1 Cor. 3:14–15)

The purpose of the inspection isn't to decide whose work has earned salvation—our salvation is sealed the moment we believe. The fire strictly determines the rewards we will receive.[2]

> ### Materials Check
>
> What kind of materials are you using in your construction? Have you paved a walkway of hospitality out front? Have you put in a door of love on humility's hinges? Have you built with the golden bricks of contentment, patience, and honesty?
>
> Just remember: your building will be inspected by eyes that can see into every crevice ... every cluttered closet ... every storeroom stuffed with straw. So don't take shortcuts. Follow God's blueprint exactly. Build your life on His foundation with materials that will withstand the blaze of His knowing eyes.

---

2. For a helpful treatment of Christian rewards, see the book *Improving Your Serve: The Art of Unselfish Living,* by Charles R. Swindoll (Waco, Tex.: Word Books, 1981), pp. 192–209.

III. Assuring a Purified Temple

Paul's third image describes the Corinthians as more than just a building. To show the high value God places on the purity of the local church, he calls them a temple.[3]

A. The facts. Paul tells the Corinthians that they are the temple of God, His shrine—and that the Holy Spirit indwells them (v. 16). As a church body and as individuals, they were supposed to be walking, breathing temples of His holiness.

B. The warning. Next, Paul warns them with the strident truth.

> If any man destroys the temple of God, God will destroy him. (v. 17a)

This is not referring to believers who commit suicide, but to those who desecrate the temple. The idea is that anybody who keeps on degrading the inner man, the part God has declared sacred, will be destroyed. The believer's spirit will be saved, but the physical body will be destroyed through an act of divine discipline. Why does God deal so harshly with those who persist in dirtying His temple?

> For the temple of God is holy, and that is what you are. (v. 17b)

Cleaning the Temple

How much time and energy do we put into cleaning up our lives? Where is our passion for purifying our hearts from every fraction of an ounce of sin's poison?

There may come a time when God says "That's enough." A patient God, yes. But He will only tolerate godlessness so long.

In this lesson we studied the three images Paul used to rebuke the Corinthians—not to entertain them, but to *warn* them. "Be a mature plant. A quality building. A pure temple." Why not take these admonitions to heart, Christian? Why not make Paul's pictures part of your life and live wholeheartedly for Jesus?

---

3. "Two different Greek words are translated 'temple' in the [New Testament].... The first is *hieron,* which means a sacred place.... The second, *naos,* refers to the sanctuary itself, containing the holy place and the holy of holies.... *Naos* is the word used here. In a sense it could be said that the Christians together constituted God's dwelling place in Corinth." From *Word Meanings in the New Testament,* by Ralph Earle (Grand Rapids, Mich.: Baker Book House, 1986), pp. 220–21.

Living Insights

In this passage of Scripture, Paul uses three rich word pictures to describe Christians. Let's sharpen our observation skills on this great text.

● The secret to good observation is the ability to ask good questions. No question is too simple or too deep—every one is important. Read 1 Corinthians 3:5–17 and jot down questions that come to mind. Then go back over the passage and begin looking for answers. You'll be amazed at how many can be found within the very verses you studied.

1 Corinthians 3:5–17

Verse: _____ Question: _____

_____

Answer: _____

_____

Verse: _____ Question: _____

_____

Answer: _____

_____

Verse: _____ Question: _____

_____

Answer: _____

_____

Verse: _____ Question: _____

_____

Answer: _____

_____

Continued on next page

57

Verse: _____ Question: _____

Answer: _____

Verse: _____ Question: _____

Answer: _____

Verse: _____ Question: _____

Answer: _____

🌿 *Living Insights*

Study Two ▰▰▰▰▰▰▰▰▰▰▰▰▰▰▰▰▰▰▰▰▰

The title of this study is "Three Pictures of You"—a title that begs us to personalize this lesson. How do the three analogies we studied describe your life?

- Spend a few minutes evaluating where you stand in each of these three areas. Ask yourself these questions: How well does this term describe me? How could I improve in this area?

A Mature Plant

_____

_____

_____

_____

_____

A Quality Building

_____

_____

_____

_____

A Pure Temple

_____

_____

_____

_____

How to Be a Very Wise Fool

1 Corinthians 3:18–4:5

History is indelibly marked by the "foolishness" of God.[1] Take the case
of Noah, for example. The Lord told him to build a three-level barge half
the length of the *Queen Mary,* larger in area than twenty basketball courts,
and as high as a four-story apartment building (Gen. 6:13–16).[2] And God
commanded him to build it hundreds of miles away from any body of water
deep enough to sustain it. Then Noah was given 120 years to complete the
ship (v. 3). Can you imagine the flak he must have endured? And yet, when
the appointed day of judgment came, the jeers were drowned in torrential
rains and floods. Only Noah, his family, and the animals he had loaded
onto the ark were spared (7:6–23). Belief in God's foolishness led to deliverance.

Consider also Joshua's conquest of Jericho. This Canaanite stronghold
had to be overthrown if the Israelites were going to take the Promised
Land. But it was locked up tighter than a nuclear test site (Josh. 6:1). How
could they get in? Should they surround the city and shoot flaming arrows
into it? Should they scale the massive stone wall and use battering rams
to break through the gates? Or should they cut off Jericho's food supply
and wait months for its inhabitants to starve to death? General Joshua
consulted with God and returned to the Israelites with this plan: The armed
men were to march around Jericho once a day for six days with seven
priests blowing rams' horns while the ark of the covenant was carried
behind them; on the seventh day, they were to circle the city seven times
and shout on command; then the wall would collapse so the army could
move in and take the city (vv. 2–10). Had Joshua lost his mind? No—he
had chosen to follow the foolishness of God; and it brought him victory
(vv. 15–25).

Throughout Scripture, God worked in ways that to us seem foolish. And
He still loves to baffle us with the unexpected, the seemingly impossible.
Just when we think we've got Him figured out, He puts a crimp in our
intellectualism, reminding us—yes, again—that in His "foolishness" lies
wisdom.

The Corinthians lived with upturned noses, breathing only the esoteric
air of their own intelligence. So Paul tells them how to be truly wise—by
trusting in the foolishness of God's wisdom.

---

1. Walter Martin develops this theme in his cassette "The Foolishness of God" (Santa Ana,
Calif.: Vision House Publishers, 1974).

2. See *The Genesis Flood,* by John C. Whitcomb, Jr., and Henry M. Morris (Grand Rapids, Mich.:
Baker Book House, 1961), pp. 10–11.

I. Two Kinds of Wisdom

We have already studied Paul's contrast between divine and human wisdom and seen that the world regards God's wisdom as absurd (1 Cor. 1:18–25). Before looking at the rest of Paul's thoughts on this subject, we will turn to James's epistle and see what he has to say about these two kinds of wisdom.

A. Divine wisdom. James shows us the first type, asking,

> Who among you is wise and understanding? Let him show by his good behavior his deeds in the gentleness of wisdom. (3:13)

God's wisdom can be seen in our behavior. It is "first pure, then peaceable, gentle, reasonable, full of mercy and good fruits, unwavering, without hypocrisy" (v. 17).

B. Human wisdom. In contrast, the second sort is full of hypocrisy. James describes it in no soft terms.

> But if you have bitter jealousy and selfish ambition in your heart, do not be arrogant and so lie against the truth. This wisdom is not that which comes down from above, but is earthly, natural, demonic. For where jealousy and selfish ambition exist, there is disorder and every evil thing. (vv. 14–16)

Unfortunately, human wisdom begs for the embrace of every mind—not just that of unbelievers. The Corinthians had embraced it. And, failing to see the real foolishness of this earthly wisdom, they refused to let it go. Though fractured and fissured, many churches today also hold on to their own wisdom.

> We look about us and see fellowships being sundered—sometimes in the name of the Holy Spirit, the Spirit of fellowship himself! It does not look as if we really believe James when he says that the spirit which promotes, tolerates and brings about divisions is of the earth (not of heaven), of the natural man (not of the Spirit of God) and of the devil (not of the Lord). We look about us and find Christians being catty and petty, as anxious to keep their end up, and to defend their rights, and so on, as the next man.[3]

II. Becoming a Fool for Christ

After explaining to the Corinthians their need to put God first and live according to His wisdom, Paul tells them how to do it. In 1 Corinthians 3:18–4:5, he gives five steps to becoming a wise fool for the Lord.

---

3. J. A. Motyer, *The Message of James: The Tests of Faith* (Downers Grove, Ill.: InterVarsity Press, 1985), p. 135.

A. Stay humble enough to keep learning. Paul starts off with a warning:

> Let no man deceive himself. If any man among you thinks that he is wise in this age, let him become foolish that he may become wise. (3:18)

The word *deceive* means "to give a false impression, whether by appearance or statement or influence." The Corinthians were self-deceived. They had the impression that they knew it all. Self-deception soon drives us to become like Nebuchadnezzar, proudly looking over our kingdoms and singing our praises for what we think we have done (Dan. 4:28–30). How wise we are in our own eyes! But Paul gives God's appraisal of that wisdom.

> For the wisdom of this world is foolishness before God. For it is written, "He is the one who catches the wise in their craftiness"; and again, "The Lord knows the reasonings of the wise, that they are useless." (1 Cor. 3:19–20)

The Lord is not impressed with Christians who live only to develop their minds. He wants us to develop genuine humility as well. This is not a call to anti-intellectualism. It's a call to the cross. As Karl A. Olsson notes:

> For Paul Christian wisdom . . . begins rather with a crucifixion, a radical humiliation. . . . The initial blinding of Paul on the Damascus road burned out his eyes and had immense significance in his subsequent life. He had to learn to see afresh. And all that he saw after that point, he saw through the prism of the Crucified. . . .
>
> This does not mean that Paul did not reason logically. . . . What it means is that his ultimate principle of coherence, that which made his thought hang together, was his crucified and risen Lord.[4]

B. Don't exalt other people. Paul gives another step to becoming a wise fool when he tells the Corinthians "let no one boast in men" (v. 21a). Exalting people perpetuates immaturity. If the Son is obscured by the shadow of another, believers will not grow. Also, idolizing people ultimately leads to a precipitous crash. Any god but the Lord is sure to fall, top-heavy, from its elevated pedestal. People-worship will limit your perspective.

> For all things belong to you, whether Paul or Apollos or Cephas or the world or life or death or things

---

4. Karl A. Olsson, *Seven Sins and Seven Virtues* (New York, N.Y.: Harper and Brothers, 1959), p. 72.

present or things to come; all things belong to you, and you belong to Christ; and Christ belongs to God. (vv. 21b–23)

As William Barclay explains:

> In verse 22, as so often happens in his letters, the march of Paul's prose suddenly takes wings and becomes a lyric of passion and poetry. The Corinthians are doing what is to Paul an inexplicable thing. They are seeking to give themselves over into the hands of some man. Paul tells them that, in point of fact, it is not they who belong to him but he who belongs to them. This identification with some party is the acceptance of slavery by those who should be kings. In fact they are masters of all things, because they belong to Christ and Christ belongs to God. The man who gives his strength and his heart to some little splinter of a party has surrendered everything to a petty thing, when he could have entered into possession of a fellowship and a love as wide as the universe. He has confined into narrow limits a life which should be limitless in its outlook.[5]

Paul then tells them the right way to treat those they respect.

> Let a man regard us in this manner, as *servants* of Christ, and *stewards* of the mysteries of God. (4:1, emphasis added)

Here the word *servant* means "an under-rower"—an oarsman on the bottom level of a vessel. Regardless of how prominent or authoritative, all believers are merely oarsmen on a ship, responsible to their captain, Jesus Christ. We are also to treat our leaders as *stewards,* managers of the affairs of God's household—the church.

A Word of Application

Have you given an under-rower the position of manning the rudder of your life? Have you given a steward the deed to your heart? If so, your ship is sure to sink . . . your heart's foundation sure to fracture.

But if you let Jesus be your Lord, He will steer you to His wisdom . . . He will scrub the pride from the walls of your heart.

---

5. William Barclay, *The Letters to the Corinthians,* rev. ed., The Daily Study Bible Series (Philadelphia, Pa.: Westminster Press, 1975), p. 35.

C. Exercise faithfulness. "It is required," says Paul, "that those who have been given a trust must prove faithful" (4:2).[6] God is not nearly as concerned with fruitfulness as He is with faithfulness. Faithfulness is what He honors. Faithfulness is what daily brings us back to the foot of His throne to ask, "Lord, how can I serve You?"

The Fruitfulness of Faithfulness

Sometimes we're so preoccupied with counting our spiritual apples and oranges that we forget to spend time watering our roots by just serving Jesus.

Try forgetting about being fruitful for a while. It will happen naturally if you let His living water soak into the depths of your soul.

D. Treat lightly others' opinions of you. Paul states his practice of this principle bluntly: "I care very little if I am judged by you or by any human court" (v. 3).[7] When we serve the Lord visibly, our every action will be judged; some will praise us, some will criticize. We should dwell on neither response or we will become like the Pharisees—intent on pleasing people while giving the impression that we are serving God.[8] Paul also says that he doesn't take his own opinion of himself too seriously:

> In fact, I do not even examine myself. I am conscious of nothing against myself, yet I am not by this acquitted. (vv. 3b–4a)

E. Leave judgment and criticism with the Lord. Explaining why he doesn't place too much stock in his and others' opinions, Paul says, "the one who examines me is the Lord" (v. 4b). "Therefore," Paul continues,

> do not go on passing judgment before the time,[9] but wait until the Lord comes who will both bring to light the things hidden in the darkness and disclose the motives of men's hearts; and then each man's praise will come to him from God. (v. 5)

Only God can judge fairly; He alone can light the things hidden in darkness ... He alone knows man's motives ... He alone has

---

6. *The NIV Study Bible* (Grand Rapids, Mich.: Zondervan Bible Publishers, 1985).

7. *The NIV Study Bible.*

8. Christ reserved His most scathing judgments for this kind of hypocrisy (see Matt. 23:13–36).

9. Paul is referring here to the Judgment Day, when each person's work—whether stubble or precious stone—will be judged by fire (see Rom. 14:10, 2 Cor. 5:10).

a clear view into our hearts. We can't see another's heart accurately—we have too many vices, inconsistencies, impurities ... too much pride in our eyes. As Jesus said in the Sermon on the Mount:

> "And why do you look at the speck that is in your brother's eye, but do not notice the log that is in your own eye? Or how can you say to your brother, 'Let me take the speck out of your eye,' and behold, the log is in your own eye? You hypocrite, first take the log out of your own eye, and then you will see clearly to take the speck out of your brother's eye." (Matt. 7:3–5)

Is there a log in your eye? Something that's keeping you from becoming a wise fool? Paul has shown us how to become one. He has said to be teachable ... not to exalt others ... to be faithful ... not to value too highly the opinions of others ... to let God be the judge. If you struggle in one of these areas, ask the Lord to help you overcome it. He will be faithful to help you (see v. 7, James 1:5). Washing the pride from your eyes, He will replace your foolishness with His wisdom.

 Living Insights

Study One ▬▬▬▬▬▬▬▬▬▬▬▬▬▬▬▬▬▬▬▬▬▬▬▬▬▬▬▬

Like the end of the first chapter, 1 Corinthians 3 concludes with comments about wisdom. Paul's main point is that the world doesn't see things the way God does. And Solomon—the wisest man who ever lived—agreed with him.

- King Solomon had much to say about wisdom. Read the first two chapters of Proverbs. In the space provided, write down the reference of each passage that talks about wisdom and summarize what each is teaching.

A Look at True Wisdom: Proverbs 1–2

Reference: _____ Summary: _____

_____

_____

Continued on next page

Study One—Continued

Reference: _____   Summary: _____

_____

_____

Reference: _____   Summary: _____

_____

_____

Reference: _____   Summary: _____

_____

_____

Reference: _____   Summary: _____

_____

_____

Reference: _____   Summary: _____

_____

_____

🐾 *Living Insights*

Study Two ━━━━━━━━━━━━━━━━━━━━━━━━━━━━━━━

Part of being a wise person is applying what you learn. After studying Solomon's writings in Proverbs, let's be wise and put them into practice.

- Think about the summaries you wrote in Study One and decide on what you can do to apply the truths you've learned. Write your ideas in the space provided.

True Wisdom Applied: Proverbs 1–2

Reference: _____   Application: _____

_____

_____

Reference: _____ Application: _____

_____

_____

Reference: _____ Application: _____

_____

_____

Reference: _____ Application: _____

_____

_____

Reference: _____ Application: _____

_____

_____

Reference: _____ Application: _____

_____

_____

Correction from a Faithful Father

1 Corinthians 4:6–14, 1 Samuel 1–4

Do you remember the last time you were spanked? It was probably more years ago than you care to recall, but try. Perhaps you were discovered in a lie or caught stealing candy from the neighborhood drugstore or sent home from school for fighting. Whatever the reason, you found yourself face-to-face with an angry parent whose look of disappointment or rage let you know that your behavior was unacceptable. Still pleading for amnesty, you turned your back—or, more likely, were firmly turned until your backside was in a vulnerable position—and winced as you felt the sting of the first stroke. Other swats followed, until your bottom throbbed like it had just been attacked by a swarm of bees. But you knew, despite your anger and excuses, that your mother or father had done the right thing.

If you're a Christian, you realize that correction doesn't stop with your earthly parents. Your heavenly Father disciplines you so that you can "share His holiness" (Heb. 12:10b). But, unlike your parents—who may have punished you wrongly at times—the Lord always chastises you for the right reason, in the right way, at the right time, and to the right degree (vv. 10–11). He never makes mistakes. And He disciplines you to show His love for you. " 'The Lord disciplines those he loves, / and he punishes everyone he accepts as a son' " (v. 6).[1]

With authority and love, Paul uses his pen as a rod to correct the wayward Corinthian Christians. Though we cannot hear the cries of these believers as they endured the pain of their reproof, we can read the stinging rebuke they received and see how it applies to us today.

I. The Corinthians' Spanking

Paul looked upon the Corinthians not just as wayward saints but as *his* disobedient children. He had planted the gospel in Corinthian soil (1 Cor. 3:6), laid the foundation for their spiritual growth (v. 10), and become their spiritual father (4:15). He had delivered them, fed them, changed their diapers, and taught them how to talk and reason. In this role, he had the right and responsibility to discipline them. In an attempt to correct the Corinthians, Paul lands a verbal rod on the Corinthians' behind so that they "might learn not to exceed what is written, in order that [none] might become arrogant in behalf of one against the other" (v. 6b).[2]

1. *The NIV Study Bible* (Grand Rapids, Mich.: Zondervan Bible Publishers, 1985).

2. Although the interpretation of this passage is difficult to pin down, Harold Mare probably comes closest to its meaning: "If [the Corinthians] learn not to go beyond the teaching of the Scripture about how they should treat God's teachers and all of God's people, then the result

Footnote continued on next page

As part of his discipline, Paul paddles the Corinthians with three
rhetorical questions that bruise their egos (v. 7). Then he grabs them
by the shoulders, looks them right in the eye, and dresses them
down with some biting sarcasm.

A. Questions that hurt. First he asks, "For who regards you as
superior?" (v. 7a). The expected answer is "No one." The Corinthian church was on equal footing with all other churches. They
weren't the least bit superior. Next, he asks, "And what do you
have that you did not receive?" (v. 7b). The answer is "Nothing."
They had heard the gospel from Paul, were saved by Christ, and
were taught by Paul and Apollos. All the good they possessed
came from another. Finally, he demands, "Why do you boast as
if you had not received it?" (v. 7c). Paul leaves them silent, egos
reeling from this stinging reproof. Like the Corinthians, we must
shun feeling superior and indispensable, always remembering
that "every good thing bestowed and every perfect gift is from
above, coming down from the Father of lights, with whom there
is no variation, or shifting shadow" (James 1:17).

B. A piercing rebuke. Their sense of superiority so soured their
testimonies that Paul felt moved to deliver a piercing rebuke
(1 Cor. 4:8–13). David Prior comments on their prideful attitude:

> At the heart of the boasting at Corinth was the con-
> viction that they were really a very successful, lively,
> mature and effective church. The Christians were sat-
> isfied with their spirituality, their leadership, and the
> general quality of their life together. They had settled

will be that they will not be conceited in taking a stand for one teacher or person over against
another." From "1 Corinthians," by Harold Mare, in *The Expositor's Bible Commentary,* 12 vols.,
ed. Frank E. Gaebelein (Grand Rapids, Mich.: Zondervan Publishing House, 1976), vol. 10,
p. 212.

down into the illusion that they had become the best they could be. They thought they had 'arrived'.[3]

So Paul punctures their inflated egos with piercing irony.

> You are already filled, you have already become rich, you have become kings without us; and I would indeed that you had become kings so that we also might reign with you. For, I think, God has exhibited us apostles last of all, as men condemned to death; because we have become a spectacle to the world, both to angels and to men. (vv. 8–9)

Here Paul calls himself and other church leaders "men condemned to death[4] ... a spectacle to the world" (v. 9b). And he contrasts himself with the Corinthians, who think they stand far above these lowly ministers. Then he describes the kinds of experiences he has endured. Notice that Paul's list begins with "To this present hour" (v. 11a). He wasn't a theoretical sufferer. He *experienced* life at the bottom of the barrel.

> To this present hour we are both hungry and thirsty, and are poorly clothed, and are roughly treated, and are homeless; and we toil, working with our own hands; when we are reviled, we bless; when we are persecuted, we endure; when we are slandered, we try to conciliate; we have become as the scum of the world, the dregs of all things, even until now. (vv. 11–13)

A Cure for Feeling Superior

There's nothing like reading the biographies of some of God's saints to cure a superiority complex.[5] You'll quickly discover what the writer of Hebrews noticed centuries ago as he surveyed the annals of history:

> Others [of God's people] were tortured, not accepting their release, in order that they might obtain a better resurrection; and others experienced mockings and scourgings, yes, also chains and imprisonment. They were stoned,

---

3. David Prior, *The Message of 1 Corinthians: Life in the Local Church* (Downers Grove, Ill.: InterVarsity Press, 1985), p. 65.

4. Ralph Earle suggests that this clause pictures " 'condemned criminals ... doomed gladiators in the arena.' " See *Word Meanings in the New Testament,* by Ralph Earle (Grand Rapids, Mich.: Baker Book House, 1986), p. 223.

5. For some revealing reading on people who lived and died for Jesus, see *Foxe's Book of Martyrs,* by John Foxe (Springdale, Pa.: Whitaker House, 1981); *Eerdman's Handbook to Christianity in America,* ed. Mark A. Noll, et al. (Grand Rapids, Mich.: William B. Eerdmans Publishing Co., 1983); and *Heritage of Freedom* (Belleville, Mich.: Lion Publishing Corp., 1984).

> they were sawn in two, they were tempted, they
> were put to death with the sword; they went
> about in sheepskins, in goatskins, being desti-
> tute, afflicted, ill-treated (men of whom the
> world was not worthy), wandering in deserts
> and mountains and caves and holes in the
> ground. (Heb. 11:35b–38)

Paul's point is clear: Believers who live for Christ will not be treated in a way that will give them superiority complexes. Paul highlights this truth not to shame the Corinthians but to admonish them—to straighten out their twisted thinking and correct their erroneous behavior (1 Cor. 4:14).[6]

II. Discipline in the Home

Paul's verbal confrontation with the Corinthian Christians has a special application to parents. Words can often correct wrongful conduct better than a well-placed rod. Certainly, the Bible encourages the rod's use in disciplining children (Prov. 13:24, 22:15), but it also promotes the use of instruction and admonition (Gen. 18:19; Deut. 6:7; Prov. 1:23, 13:18, 15:31–32; Eph. 6:4). When we use one method to the neglect of the other—or spurn both altogether—we and our children suffer. The book of 1 Samuel gives us an excellent illustration.

A. Eli's example. Unlike Eli, who was a highly respected priest dedicated to God (1:9–18, 2:18–21), his sons Hophni and Phinehas were "worthless men [who] did not know the Lord" (2:12). Their blasphemous arrogance can, in part, be traced back to their father's failure to discipline them adequately. The text says that Eli " 'did not rebuke[7] [his sons]' " (3:13b). He did nothing to dim the fiery passions that burned out of control in them, nothing to weaken their rebellious wills which stood hard and fast against God. Inevitably, the rod of discipline was taken from Eli's lethargic hands by the Lord—and His discipline was not only swift, it was final (3:11–14, 4:11).

B. Eli's mistakes. Two of Eli's glaring mistakes are spotlighted in 2:22–23.

> Now Eli was very old; and he heard all that his sons
> were doing to all Israel, and how they lay with the

---

6. The Greek word for *shame, entrepō,* conveys the idea of turning against oneself, while the word *admonish, noutheteō* in the Greek, means "to place into the mind." Paul did not wish to turn the Corinthians against themselves but to encourage a change of heart.

7. The Hebrew word for *rebuke* means "to weaken." The Greek term means "to place into the mind a direct confrontation."

women who served at the doorway of the tent of meeting. And he said to them, "Why do you do such things, the evil things that I hear from all these people?"

First, notice that Eli knew about his son's sins only by hearsay. He didn't really know his sons. He hadn't studied them enough to develop a deep, parental understanding of them. Second, he asked the wrong question: Why? He knew why—they were sinners. Asking why results in blame-shifting, not healthy confrontation. To help them right their wrong, parents need to tell their children *what* they have done . . . and what God thinks about what they have done. They must also make clear what it will take to reconcile the wrong. Eli's poor approach to discipline bred a recalcitrant response from his sons: "But they would not listen to the voice of their father" (v. 25b).

Discipline in Your Home

Eli.

Paul.

Both were fathers, but with very different approaches to discipline.

Parents, whose approach do you model? Like Eli, are you blind to your child's weaknesses and wayward ways— dumb, unable to give a needed word of rebuke? Or are you like Paul, clearly seeing the spiritual condition of your children's hearts and quickly speaking up to confront their wrongs?

True love disciplines (Heb. 12:7; Prov. 3:12, 13:24). Do you love your children? Then discipline them diligently and consistently. Depending on the presence or absence of proper discipline, your child will be either a delight and a comfort to you (Prov. 29:17) or a source of shame (v. 15).[8]

---

8. For further study on child discipline, consult *Dare to Discipline* (Wheaton, Ill.: Tyndale House Publishers, 1970) and *The Strong-Willed Child* (Wheaton, Ill.: Tyndale House Publishers, 1978), by James Dobson; *You and Your Child,* by Charles R. Swindoll (Nashville, Tenn.: Thomas Nelson Publishers, 1977); and the study guide *You and Your Child,* coauthored by Ken Gire, from the Bible-teaching ministry of Charles R. Swindoll (Fullerton, Calif.: Insight for Living, 1986), pp. 27–43.

Living Insights

First Corinthians 4:6–14 is loaded with descriptive words. A master with his pen, the apostle Paul conveyed deep feelings through his choice of words. Let's review this passage with the specific intent of examining these descriptions.

● Reread 1 Corinthians 4:6–14. In the chart below, write down the words that are especially descriptive of people—words like *rich, kings, fools, hungry.* Pay special attention to the meanings Paul had in mind when he wrote them, and think about what these descriptions say to you.

1 Corinthians 4:6–14	
Paul's Definitions	Your Interpretations
Descriptive word: _____	
Descriptive word: _____	
Descriptive word: _____	

Continued on next page

Paul's Definitions	Your Interpretations
Descriptive word: _____	
Descriptive word: _____	
Descriptive word: _____	
Descriptive word: _____	

Paul's Definitions	Your Interpretations
Descriptive word: _____	
Descriptive word: _____	
Descriptive word: _____	
Descriptive word: _____	

Continued on next page

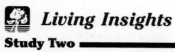 *Living Insights*

This lesson closed with some strong statements of application. How do *you* handle the issues raised in this study? Take a few minutes to think about each of the questions listed below; then record your answers.

● How do I deal with arrogant people?

_____

_____

_____

● How do I respond when someone confronts a wrong in my life?

_____

_____

_____

● How do I confront someone else about their wrongdoing?

_____

_____

_____

● Our attitude toward others often affects their actions toward us. What sort of attitude have I been conveying lately?

_____

_____

_____

● How can I improve my attitude?

_____

_____

_____

How to Handle a Scandal
1 Corinthians 5

As Christians, we are island dwellers surrounded by a polluted sea that continually beats upon our shores.

This presents a problem that tugs at us day and night . . . in our tropical, fertile seasons as well as in parched, barren times. How can we insulate ourselves from the world without isolating ourselves from people? How can we stay pure when the world's contaminated waters constantly lap upon the beaches of our lives?

Many believers skirt this problem by giving in. They leave the purity of their islands and dive into the world's sea.

In 1 Corinthians 5, we read about a member of the church at Corinth who had done just that. He had surrendered to corruption's siren call and plunged into a sea of scandalous sin.

In this passage Paul rebukes not only this man's sin but the Corinthians' sin as well. The Corinthians were proud of their too liberal tolerance, which blinded them to the need for a reprimand. Paul shows them the seriousness of this complacency and teaches them that true love is tenacious—especially in the face of a scandal.[1]

I. The Scandal

Moral pollution had seeped into the Corinthian church, and now the news was out:

> It is actually reported that there is immorality among you, and immorality of such a kind as does not exist even among the Gentiles, that someone has his father's wife. (v. 1)

We can make three significant observations from this verse. First, the sin was well known. Paul says, "It is actually reported." This was no secret scandal—it was front page news in the *Corinthian Times*. Second, the sin was incestuous. The man was committing this abomination with his stepmother. And third, while the Christians were complacent, the godless Gentiles were repulsed by this sin, a sin that the Romans prohibited by law.

---

1. "Unless someone in the church decides to go lovingly to the person involved in the scandal with the object of establishing the truth, effecting righteousness and seeking to bring about reconciliation, *every single member in the church who is aware of the situation is sinning every moment—is in fact a participator in the sin of the 'identified sinner' in one way or another. The church is sinning by avoiding corrective church discipline.*" From *Healing the Wounded: The Costly Love of Church Discipline,* by John White and Ken Blue, foreword by Ray C. Stedman (Downers Grove, Ill.: InterVarsity Press, 1985), p. 66.

II. Two Responses

Surprisingly, the Corinthians were not repulsed. They had been wading in the stagnant waters of pride so long that they failed to see the real filth of this situation. So Paul talks to them about their reaction, tells them his feelings concerning the scandal, and then explains how situations like this should be handled.

A. Prideful permissiveness. Paul rebukes the Corinthians with bold honesty:

> And you have become arrogant, and have not mourned instead. (v. 2a)

They had adopted a destructive view of grace. Salvation in Christ, they thought, permits believers to do what they want. They should have grieved over their brother's sin as a mother laments the death of her child. Instead, they accepted it and were indifferent to his need for rebuke.

God's View of Sin

How do you view sin? Like the Corinthians, do you shrug it off arrogantly? Or do you see it as God sees it . . . do you let it break your heart (see Jer. 23:9–10, Ezek. 6:9, Ps. 78:40)?

B. Caring judgment. Paul takes a stand against the majority opinion in the Corinthian congregation, saying,

> For I, on my part, though absent in body but present in spirit, have already judged him who has so committed this, as though I were present.[2] (1 Cor. 5:3)

Paul realized that for the good of the sinning brother and the rest of the congregation, someone must take a stand—discipline must be carried out.

III. Paul's Counsel

In the remainder of the chapter, Paul gives the Corinthians specific instructions for the situation at hand, as well as guidelines for the future.

A. Handling the Corinthians' case. Paul doesn't appeal to church traditions or constitutions. Neither does he call on church leaders to wield their authority. Instead, he exhorts the Corinthian congregation to apply correction in the name and power of Jesus Christ (vv. 4–5). If the church fails to do so, they invite the moral pollution to stay, jeopardizing the spiritual

---

2. Paul's judgment of the believer involved in incest is not the hypocritical self-righteousness that Jesus condemns in Matthew 7:1–5. Rather, Paul's condemnation is based on the Bible's teaching to discern between good and evil and act accordingly (vv. 6, 15–20; John 7:24; Phil. 3:2; 1 Thess. 5:21–22; 1 John 4:1–6).

purity of the entire congregation. In verse 5, Paul gives them three specific instructions for disciplining a sinning believer.

1. **"Deliver such a one to Satan."** The Corinthian church is to excommunicate sinning Christians, releasing them into Satan's domain—the world (compare vv. 2, 13). Outside the spiritual protection of the church, they will be unable to repel the attacks of Satan, who seeks to destroy the body of Christ (1 Pet. 5:8).

2. **"For the destruction of his flesh."** This phrase may include physical death (see 1 Cor. 11:30, 1 John 5:16), but, more than likely, it refers to defeating a sinner's fleshly desires by letting Satan push those passions to extremes, creating such an anguish in the sinner that his lust is destroyed.

3. **"That his spirit may be saved."** The goal of this harsh discipline is not punishment—this is only the means to an end, and that end is restoration. As William Barclay explains:

> Always at the back of punishment and discipline in the early Church there is the conviction that they must seek not to break but to make the man who has sinned. . . . Discipline should never be exercised for the satisfaction of the person who exercises it, but always for the mending of the person who has sinned and for the sake of the Church. Discipline must never be vengeful; it must always be curative.[3]

Paul commands churches to lovingly correct, not vindictively punish, members who persist in sinning (compare Matt. 18:15–17). Once a change of mind and heart is gained, congregations should welcome prodigals home with open arms (Luke 15:20–24; compare 2 Cor. 2:6–8).

B. Stopping sin's spread. In a sense, believers do live on islands—set apart to Christ. But, as John Donne says,

> "No man is an island, entire of itself; every man is a
> piece of the continent, a part of the main."[4]

Because we are all part of the body of Christ, we directly affect each other for good or for bad.

3. William Barclay, *The Letters to the Corinthians,* rev. ed., The Daily Study Bible Series (Philadelphia, Pa.: Westminster Press, 1975), pp. 44–46.

4. As quoted by Thomas Merton in *No Man Is an Island* (New York, N.Y.: Harcourt Brace Jovanovich, 1955), p. xxiii.

Do you not know that a little leaven leavens the whole
lump of dough? (v. 6b)[5]

As yeast invades every part of a bread, so one Christian's sin
can corrupt an entire congregation (v. 8). So Paul tells them:

Clean out the old leaven, that you may be a new
lump, just as you are in fact unleavened. (v. 7a)

Paul reminds the Corinthians of their position in Christ (see
2 Cor. 5:17, Rom. 6:1–12), and he encourages them to put shoe
leather to this knowledge and start living like the new, "unleavened" creatures they are. Christ's sacrifice should motivate them
toward purity, because He paid a dear price to free them from
sin.

For Christ our Passover also has been sacrificed. Let
us therefore celebrate the feast, not with old leaven,
nor with the leaven of malice and wickedness, but
with the unleavened bread of sincerity and truth.
(vv. 7b–8)

Celebrating the Feast

On the day before the Passover feast, the law said that
the Jew must light a candle to search the house for leaven,
and that every bit must be cast out.

Have you tried to enjoy the feast of fellowship with
Christ before taking a candle and examining your heart for
sin? Even "small" sins? Because sin, like leaven, can start
out small, but it will eventually permeate everything it
touches.

Do as the Jews did. Hunt down that sin and repent of
it. Ask God to purify you so you can start celebrating the
feast of new life "with the unleavened bread of sincerity
and truth" (v. 8b; see also 1 John 1:9).

C. Dealing with similar situations. Paul finishes his instructions with two points we would do well to remember.

1. Who should we stay away from? Trying to clear up any
confusion, Paul tells them:

I wrote you in my letter not to associate with
immoral people; I did not at all mean with the

---

5. "Paul quotes an old proverb: 'A little leaven leavens all the dough.' To regular readers of
the KJV the term 'leaven' is familiar. But many readers of the Bible today might not be aware
of the fact that 'leaven' means 'yeast.' . . . It is true that 'leaven' has become deeply ingrained
in our language as a symbol of evil, although it is sometimes used for a good influence.
Basically it means what affects the whole group or society." From *Word Meanings in the New
Testament,* by Ralph Earle (Grand Rapids, Mich.: Baker Book House, 1986), p. 225.

immoral people of this world, or with the covetous and swindlers, or with idolaters; for then
you would have to go out of the world. But actually, I wrote to you not to associate with any
so-called brother if he should be an immoral person, or covetous, or an idolater, or a reviler, or
a drunkard, or a swindler—not even to eat with
such a one. (vv. 9–11)

As island dwellers, we can't get away from the world's immoral sea. In fact, we shouldn't even try to isolate ourselves
from it. But when it comes to defiant believers who habitu-
ally swim in the sin around them, we are told to keep them
off our shores (v. 11b).

   2. Who should we discipline? Church discipline is for Christians who stubbornly continue to sin.

For what have I to do with judging outsiders? Do
you not judge those who are within the church?
But those who are outside, God judges. Remove
the wicked man from among yourselves.
(vv. 12–13)

Scrub Brush or Fishing Pole?

     Many of us are trying to clean up the world's fish-
bowl when all God asks us to do is fish.
     Jesus says, " 'Follow Me, and I will make you fishers
of men' " (Matt. 4:19). Not cleaners of fishbowls—
fishers of men!
     If you've been spending your time trying to scour
the world, put down your scrub brush . . . pick up your
fishing pole . . . and go for the fish!

IV. Some Lasting Principles

Paul's discussion covers a lot of ground, so let's summarize his
thoughts in a way we won't easily forget.

   **A. Overlooking flagrant sin is not gracious but danger-
ous.** Just as ignoring a bulge in your tire or a rattlesnake in
your yard can result in disaster, so allowing a sinning believer
to go uncorrected can destroy a church. We dare not allow
wrong to go unchecked.

   **B. Rebuking sinning believers is not optional but es-
sential.** Both God and the world expect our churches to be
bastions of holiness. But when sin defiantly breaks out within
even one of our churches, the Lord is dishonored, His Church
defamed, and the world dismayed.

C. Dealing with sinful situations should not be punitive but remedial. James tells us:

> My brethren, if any among you strays from the truth, and one turns him back, let him know that he who turns a sinner from the error of his way will save his soul from death, and will cover a multitude of sins. (James 5:19–20)

We are not to be vultures, preying on fallen Christians. We should, however, be like divine physicians, restoring those members who are out of joint with the body of Christ (Gal. 6:1).

D. Correcting disorders is not external but internal. Christian discipline is strictly a family matter; it's to be carried out *by* believers and *for* believers. But church correction would never have to occur if Christians would keep their private worlds centered around the Lord rather than themselves. Are your toes wet from playing "innocent" games in the polluted sea around you? Or are you soaked, head to toe, from riding its waves? As long as you're on this side of eternity, it's not too late to dry off and plant your feet firmly on solid ground (see Ps. 40:1–2).

 Living Insights

Study One ━━━━━━━━━━━━━━━━━━━━━

By now it is clear that the Corinthian church was far from perfect. This group of believers had some serious problems. But the real tragedy is that this passage also hits *us* close to home.

- Earlier in this study guide we tried our hand at paraphrasing. Let's return to that helpful method. In your own words, write the thirteen verses of 1 Corinthians 5, bringing out the meaning and emotion of the text. Work slowly so you will be able to glean the most from this important passage.

1 Corinthians 5

_____

_____

_____

_____

_____

_____

_____

_____

_____

_____

_____

_____

_____

_____

_____

_____

Living Insights

Study Two ██

Are you involved in a church in your community? If so, you are responsible for helping your church stay away from the problems the Corinthian church had.

- What are some of the similarities and differences between your church and the Corinthian church? How can you keep the problems they experienced from happening to your congregation? Answer these questions in the space provided below.

My Church and the Corinthian Church

_____

_____

_____

_____

_____

_____

_____

_____

_____

_____

To Sue or Not to Sue

1 Corinthians 6:1–11

We live in a lawsuit-crazed society. In the United States alone, "over 200,000 civil suits were filed in the federal courts in one recent 12-month period. Some 610,000 lawyers (their number is increasing) are handling them. In 1977, more than 12 million suits were filed in the state courts."[1] Each year the number of cases filed in both federal and state courts grows dramatically.

What we see today is nothing new. In ancient Greece, home of the world's first democracy, the courts were brimming with activity.

> [The Greeks] were characteristically a litigious people. The law courts were one of their chief entertainments.... In a Greek city every man was more or less a lawyer and spent a very great part of his time either deciding or listening to law cases.[2]

Corinth, with its metropolitan atmosphere, international trade centers, and close proximity to Athens—the lawsuit capital of Greece—couldn't help becoming polluted by litigation mania. Unfortunately, the church in Corinth also became contaminated by the same obsession—an obsession that flourishes in Christian circles today.

In 1 Corinthians 6:1–11, Paul identifies the problem plaguing the Corinthian Christians and exposes its source, offering a workable solution not only for these believers but also for Christians today.

I. The Problem

Imitating the pagans around them, the Corinthian Christians took their disputes to the civil courts, where unbelievers judged their cases (1 Cor. 6:1, 6–7).[3] Notice Paul's indignant reaction to this practice:

> Does any one of you, when he has a case against his neighbor, dare to go to law before the unrighteous, and not before the saints ... but brother goes to law with brother, and that before unbelievers? Actually, then, it is already a defeat for you, that you have lawsuits with one another. (vv. 1, 6–7a)

---

1. Warren W. Wiersbe, *Be Wise* (Wheaton, Ill.: Victor Books, 1983), p. 68.

2. William Barclay, *The Letters to the Corinthians,* rev. ed., The Daily Study Bible Series (Philadelphia, Pa.: Westminster Press, 1975), pp. 49–50.

3. "In speaking of Christians taking other Christians to court, Paul does not specify any criminal cases because he teaches elsewhere that these must be handled by the state (Rom. 13:3, 4). In the expression *pragma echōn* ('having a lawsuit or dispute'), Paul means to include different kinds of property cases [1 Cor. 6:7]." From "1 Corinthians," by Harold Mare, in *The Expositor's Bible Commentary,* 12 vols., ed. Frank E. Gaebelein (Grand Rapids, Mich.: Zondervan Publishing House, 1976), vol. 10, p. 221.

Unbelievers must have had a field day watching these Christians call each other to the witness stand. Their silly display of selfishness must have had the unsaved sneering at Christianity even more than usual. No wonder Paul tells them that regardless of the outcome of their suits, they are already losers, because they've warred against each other in front of unbelievers (v. 7a). Who will believe that Christianity is the answer to life's problems when those who follow Christ run to the world to settle their differences?

A Note of Clarification

Paul is not attacking the courts . . . he's not antigovernment (see Rom. 13:1–7).[4] His concern is not the public court system itself but the believers who use it as a floor for their squabbles. When this happens, the witness of the Church is weakened and unbelievers scoff and jeer.

As a defendant of Christianity, how's your witness? Is your life any different from the plaintiff's?

Remember, unbelievers are watching you. Every day you are on trial.

II. The Solution

Next, Paul moves his discussion from the problem to the solution. The Corinthians had failed to apply the facts of their Christian identity and inheritance, so Paul walks them through these truths one more time.

A. Position of the saints. Paul reminds them of who they are in Christ.

> Or do you not know that the saints will judge the
> world? (1 Cor. 6:2a)

In Christ, they are somebody, and one day they will join the Lord to rule over the earth (Jude 14–15; Rev. 2:26–27, 3:21, 20:4). Based on this, he asks the Corinthians, "Are you not competent to constitute the smallest law courts?" (1 Cor. 6:2b). "Of course!" Paul practically shouts between the lines. They didn't have to be legal experts to resolve most of their disputes. Once they really understood their position in Christ and the appropriate biblical principles, they had the essentials. All they needed to do was apply them. And the same holds true for us today. Paul asks another question,

> Do you not know that we shall judge angels? How
> much more, matters of this life? (v. 3)

4. Paul's outburst against the Corinthians had nothing to do with any mistrust in the courts' integrity or propriety. See *The Message of 1 Corinthians: Life in the Local Church,* by David Prior (Downers Grove, Ill.: InterVarsity Press, 1985), p. 107.

With authority over both heaven and earth, certainly we, like the ancient saints of Corinth, have the right and obligation to resolve our own squabbles.

B. Judgment on the judges. In verses 4–5, Paul uses sarcasm to gavel his point into the Corinthians' minds.

> If then you have law courts dealing with matters of this life, do you appoint them as judges who are of no account in the church? I say this to your shame. Is it so, that there is not among you one wise man who will be able to decide between his brethren?

Paul isn't putting down unbelievers when he says "judges who are of no account in the church." He just wants to show that the unsaved don't have the spiritual insight available to believers. Asking a non-Christian for godly advice is like seeking marriage counseling from someone who's been divorced several times or entering a writing contest with judges who can't read. The idea is not only absurd, but, as Paul says, it's shameful (v. 5).

C. Response of the recipients. Like an ice cube on a sensitive tooth, Paul continues to chill their pride. In verses 7–8 he shows them the right ways to respond: "Why not rather be wronged? Why not rather be defrauded?" (v. 7b). If fellow Christians slander us, we should suffer the wrong rather than sue them in court. If believers defraud us, we should take the loss instead of pressing charges. Tough teaching to apply! Like the Corinthians, we want to stand up for our rights and fight for our reputations and possessions. But Jesus makes our responsibility clear:

> "You have heard that it was said, 'An eye for an eye, and a tooth for a tooth.' But I say to you, do not resist him who is evil; but whoever slaps you on your right cheek, turn to him the other also. And if anyone wants to sue you, and take your shirt, let him have your coat also." (Matt. 5:38–40)

The Corinthians violated this teaching: "On the contrary, you yourselves wrong and defraud, and that your brethren" (1 Cor. 6:8). Not only did they refuse to turn the other cheek, but they also demanded eye-for-eye, tooth-for-tooth restitution.

Haughty or Humble?

Are you a vengeful person—the kind that demands an eye for an eye . . . looks for fights . . . judges with a critical heart? The root of this attitude is pride. Solomon once said: "Pride goes before destruction, / And a haughty spirit before stumbling" (Prov. 16:18).

> Or are you humble? When slapped on one cheek, do
> you turn the other? Remember, "The reward of humility
> and the fear of the Lord / Are riches, honor and life" (22:4).

III. The Reminder

In 1 Corinthians 6:9–11, Paul shifts the focus from the believers'
position in the Lord to their inheritance. His point is that when we
fight with fellow believers over earthly goods, we cheapen our heavenly riches and act like unbelievers, who will never have such a
legacy.

A. No inheritance for the unrighteous. Once again, Paul
reminds the Corinthians of a truth they already knew.

> Or do you not know that the unrighteous shall not
> inherit the kingdom of God? Do not be deceived;
> neither fornicators, nor idolaters, nor adulterers, nor
> effeminate, nor homosexuals, nor thieves, nor the
> covetous, nor drunkards, nor revilers, nor swindlers,
> shall inherit the kingdom of God. (vv. 9–10)

B. No unrighteousness for the heirs. Paul adds,

> And such were some of you; but you were washed,
> but you were sanctified, but you were justified in the
> name of the Lord Jesus Christ, and in the Spirit of
> our God. (v. 11)

The Corinthians knew their past was riddled with vice. But in
Jesus, they were a new people with a new moral code, a new
mind-set, a new family, a new inheritance, and a new authority.
So how could they even think of handling their disagreements
as they did when they were unsaved?

IV. The Application

The Corinthians failed to practice what they knew was right. Let's
apply what *we* know is right, so we won't make the same mistakes
the Corinthians did.

**A. A lawsuit is permissible when the issue does not
involve a local church or fellow Christian.** Paul isn't
talking about cases where one of the opposing parties is non-
Christian. However, in legal issues—as in life—believers should
always allow biblical values to direct their every decision.

**B. A lawsuit is permissible when our motive is not pride
but justice.** The courtroom should never be used as a floor
for our selfishness; instead, we should strive to reflect God's
righteous standards.

C. A lawsuit is permissible when the issue does not bring shame to Christ's name or Church. As Christians, glorifying God should be the top priority in everything we do.

D. A lawsuit is permissible when we are absolutely confident that it is in God's will. The best way to determine this is to spend time in His Word and in prayer.

The Greatest Offense

Ever since Eden, we have offended God more deeply than anyone . . . for anything, because man has repeatedly rejected, despised, and spat on His offer of unbroken fellowship. But instead of taking away the sun forever or sending another flood or withholding the very breath of life, He gave His Son to bear the penalty for our sins—just because He loves us (John 3:16, 1 John 4:9–10).

How will you respond to such grace? Will you reject it . . . again? If you do, He will have to declare you guilty. But if you accept His gift, you'll forever be seen as innocent in His eyes (see Ps. 103:12, 1 John 1:9).

 Living Insights

Study One

Wow! We've really gone through a lot of material in our twelve studies on 1 Corinthians. Let's take a second look at the lessons we've been through and review some of the key issues to help these truths sink in.

● Listed below are the titles of the twelve lessons in this series. After reviewing your study guide, list one key *truth* from each lesson.

Strong Reproofs for a Scandalous Church

Once Corinthians, Now Californians _____

_____

_____

From Riches to Rags _____

_____

_____

How to Split a Church _____

_____

Human Intellect versus Divine Wisdom _____

_____

Profound Simplicity _____

_____

The Hidden Depths of God _____

_____

The Pigpen Christian _____

_____

Three Pictures of You _____

_____

How to Be a Very Wise Fool _____

_____

Correction from a Faithful Father _____

_____

How to Handle a Scandal _____

_____

Continued on next page

To Sue or Not to Sue _____

_____

_____

Living Insights

Let's continue to review our lessons in 1 Corinthians. This time, however, let's shift our attention to the application part of our studies.

- Flip back through the pages of your study guide and pinpoint one key *application* you're practicing as a result of our study.

Strong Reproofs for a Scandalous Church

Once Corinthians, Now Californians _____

_____

_____

From Riches to Rags _____

_____

_____

How to Split a Church _____

_____

_____

Human Intellect versus Divine Wisdom _____

_____

_____

Profound Simplicity _____

_____

_____

The Hidden Depths of God _____

_____

_____

The Pigpen Christian _____

_____

_____

Three Pictures of You _____

_____

_____

How to Be a Very Wise Fool _____

_____

_____

Correction from a Faithful Father _____

_____

_____

How to Handle a Scandal _____

_____

_____

To Sue or Not to Sue _____

_____

_____

Books for Probing Further

There is one vice of which no man in the world is free; which every one in the world loathes when he sees it in someone else; and of which hardly any people, except Christians, ever imagine that they are guilty themselves....

The vice I am talking of is Pride or Self-Conceit: and the virtue opposite to it, in Christian morals, is called Humility. ... The essential vice, the utmost evil, is Pride. Unchastity, anger, greed, drunkenness, and all that, are mere fleabites in comparison: it was through Pride that the devil became the devil: Pride leads to every other vice: it is the complete anti-God state of mind.[1]

The Corinthian Christians—those who had been saved by divine grace from the cesspool of their pagan lives—had almost perfected that "anti-God state of mind." They were so masterful at their craft that they deceived themselves into thinking they were the cream of the Christian crop. Amazingly, they arrived at this conclusion in spite of their petty squabbles, vindictive accusations, and sexual permissiveness. By failing to take an honest look at themselves, they were destroying their fellowship as well as their witness in Corinth. So Paul wrote them a letter that mirrored the hard truth.

It's easy for us to read 1 Corinthians and pass judgment on those first-century believers. But if we were really honest with ourselves, we would have to admit that this letter has much to say to us. Maybe you shifted uneasily in your chair as you saw flaws in your character or behavior reflected in 1 Corinthians. Or maybe you came to grips with some truths you had not understood before. If this letter has sparked a desire to delve deeper into the Corinthian issues, then these books will be a helpful starting point for you. We hope they will enable you to see yourself more clearly ... and encourage you to be molded into the image of Christ.

Bridges, Jerry. *True Fellowship.* Colorado Springs, Colo.: NavPress, 1985. If the Corinthians lacked anything, it was *koinōnía*—Christian fellowship born out of a deep love for God and His people. Jerry Bridges takes a fresh and biblical view of fellowship, explaining what it is, what it costs, and how it can become as natural to our lives as breathing.

Griffiths, Michael. *The Example of Jesus.* Downers Grove, Ill.: InterVarsity Press, 1985. It's one thing to say "Follow Christ's example" but quite

---

1. C. S. Lewis, *Mere Christianity,* rev. and enl. (New York, N.Y.: Macmillan Publishing Co., 1952), pp. 108–9.

another to understand what that means and how it can be done in the twentieth century. Some of the Corinthians claimed Christ as their leader (1 Cor. 1:12), but their walk didn't back up their talk. This book shows what genuine conformity to Christ is all about. The author's perspective may sometimes surprise us, but it will not fail to inspire our growth toward Christlikeness.

Guinness, Os. *The Gravedigger File: Papers on the Subversion of the Modern Church.* Downers Grove, Ill.: InterVarsity Press, 1983. In our study of 1 Corinthians, we saw many of the pagan ideas and standards that infiltrated and crippled the church at Corinth. However, we often fail to see the non-Christian influences that have seeped through the cracks of *our* churches and lives, polluting our thoughts, feelings, and actions. These contaminants are exposed in this book, and a mop-up plan is proposed.

Sanders, J. Oswald. *In Pursuit of Maturity.* Grand Rapids, Mich.: Zondervan Publishing House, 1986. What kind of changes does the pursuit of maturity involve? Why should we commit ourselves to this difficult task? J. Oswald Sanders answers these questions and many more in this insightful and encouraging book.

White, John, and Ken Blue. *Healing the Wounded: The Costly Love of Church Discipline.* Foreword by Ray C. Stedman. Downers Grove, Ill.: InterVarsity Press, 1985. The Corinthian church's complacency in the face of a brother's sin led to shame for the whole congregation. This same fate still falls on churches that fail to administer discipline when they need to. The authors tackle this issue head-on, giving us a compassionate, biblical look at a topic that is too often ignored.

Woodbridge, John D., ed. *Renewing Your Mind in a Secular World.* Chicago, Ill.: Moody Press, 1985. In 1 Corinthians 1–2, Paul makes it clear that the depths of God's wisdom are available to all believers. But many of us are stuck perceiving life through the world's shallow eyes. This volume shows us how we can move beyond the world's mind-set to the hidden depths of God's wisdom so that we can affect the world with the deep, deep love of Jesus.

Acknowledgments

Insight for Living is grateful for kind permission to quote from the following source:

Barclay, William. *The Letters to the Corinthians.* Revised edition. The Daily Study Bible Series. Philadelphia, Pa.: Westminster Press; Edinburgh, Scotland: Saint Andrew Press, 1975.

Insight for Living
Cassette Tapes
STRONG REPROOFS FOR A SCANDALOUS CHURCH
A STUDY OF 1 CORINTHIANS 1:1–6:11

Ancient Corinth . . . wealthy . . . busy . . . intellectual . . . sensual . . . godless. A good place for a church. But what happens when the bright light of Christ's gospel is darkened by believers who succumb to the world system around them?

This is what happened to the church at Corinth. The apostle Paul had strong words for this stubborn body of carnal saints. Here are twelve messages based on the first part of Paul's first letter to that Corinthian church—timely reproofs for all Christians living in a godless society that desperately needs Jesus' transforming message.

			U.S.	Canada
SRS	CS	Cassette series—includes album cover	$34.50	$43.75
		Individual cassettes—include messages		
		A and B	5.00	6.35

These prices are effective as of January 1988 and are subject to change without notice.

SRS 1-A: ***Once Corinthians, Now Californians***—Acts 18:1–11, 1 Corinthians
     B: ***From Riches to Rags***—1 Corinthians 1:1–9

SRS 2-A: ***How to Split a Church***—1 Corinthians 1:10–17
     B: ***Human Intellect versus Divine Wisdom***—1 Corinthians 1:18–25

SRS 3-A: ***Profound Simplicity***—1 Corinthians 1:26–2:5
     B: ***The Hidden Depths of God***—1 Corinthians 2:6–16

SRS 4-A: ***The Pigpen Christian***—1 Corinthians 2:14–3:4, Luke 15:11–32
     B: ***Three Pictures of You***—1 Corinthians 3:5–17

SRS 5-A: ***How to Be a Very Wise Fool***—1 Corinthians 3:18–4:5
     B: ***Correction from a Faithful Father***—1 Corinthians 4:6–14,
       1 Samuel 1–4

SRS 6-A: ***How to Handle a Scandal***—1 Corinthians 5
     B: ***To Sue or Not to Sue***—1 Corinthians 6:1–11

How to Order by Mail

Ordering is easy and convenient. Simply mark on the order form whether you want the series or individual tapes, including the quantity you desire. Tear out the order form and mail it with your payment to the appropriate address on the bottom of the form. We will process your order as promptly as we can.

United States orders: If you wish your order to be shipped first-class for faster delivery, please add 10 percent of the total order amount (not including California sales tax). Otherwise, please allow four to six weeks for delivery by fourth-class mail. We accept personal checks, money orders, Visa, and Master-Card in payment for materials. Unfortunately, we are unable to offer invoicing or COD orders.

Canadian orders: Please add 7 percent of your total order for first-class postage and allow approximately four weeks for delivery. For our listeners in British Columbia, a 6 percent sales tax must also be added to the total of all tape orders (not including postage). For further information, please contact our office at (604) 272-5811. We accept personal checks, money orders, Visa, or MasterCard in payment for materials. Unfortunately, we are unable to offer invoicing or COD orders.

Overseas orders: If you live outside the United States or Canada, please allow six to ten weeks for delivery by surface mail. If you would like your order sent airmail, the delivery time may be reduced. Whether you choose surface or airmail delivery, postage costs must be added to the amount of purchase and included with your order. Please use the following chart to determine the correct postage. Due to fluctuating currency rates, we can accept only personal checks made payable in U.S. funds, international money orders, Visa, or MasterCard in payment for materials.

Type of Postage	Cassettes
Surface	10% of total order
Airmail	25% of total order

For Faster Service, Order by Telephone

To purchase using Visa or MasterCard, you are welcome to use our **toll-free** number between the hours of 8:30 A.M. and 4:00 P.M., Pacific time, Monday through Friday. The number is **1-800-772-8888,** and it may be used anywhere in the United States except California, Hawaii, and Alaska. Telephone orders from these states and overseas are handled through our Sales Department at (714) 870-9161. Canadian residents should call (604) 272-5811. We are unable to accept collect calls.

Our Guarantee

Our cassettes are guaranteed for ninety days against faulty performance or breakage due to a defect in the tape. For best results, please be sure your tape recorder is in good operating condition and is cleaned regularly.

Note: To cover processing and handling, there is a $10 fee for *any* returned check.

Order Form

SRS CS represents the entire *Strong Reproofs for a Scandalous Church* series, while SRS 1–6 are the individual tapes included in the series.

Series or Tape	Unit Price U.S.	Canada	Quantity	Amount
SRS CS	$34.50	$43.75		$
SRS 1	5.00	6.35		
SRS 2	5.00	6.35		
SRS 3	5.00	6.35		
SRS 4	5.00	6.35		
SRS 5	5.00	6.35		
SRS 6	5.00	6.35		
Subtotal				
Sales tax *6% for orders delivered in California or British Columbia*				
Postage *7% in Canada; overseas residents see "How to Order by Mail"*				
10% optional first-class shipping and handling *U.S. residents only*				
Gift to Insight for Living *Tax-deductible in the U.S. and Canada*				
Total amount due *Please do not send cash.*				$

If there is a balance: ☐ apply it as a donation ☐ please refund

Form of payment:

☐ Check or money order made payable to Insight for Living

☐ Credit card (circle one): Visa MasterCard

Card Number _____ Expiration Date _____

Signature _____
We cannot process your credit card purchase without your signature.

Name _____

Address _____

City _____

State/Province_____ Zip/Postal Code _____

Country _____

Telephone (_____)_____ Radio Station ___ ___ ___ ___
If questions arise concerning your order, we may need to contact you.

Mail this order form to the Sales Department at one of these addresses:
Insight for Living, Post Office Box 4444, Fullerton, CA 92634
Insight for Living Ministries, Post Office Box 2510, Vancouver, BC, Canada V6B 3W7

Order Form

SRS CS represents the entire *Strong Reproofs for a Scandalous Church* series, while SRS 1–6 are the individual tapes included in the series.

Series or Tape	Unit Price U.S.	Canada	Quantity	Amount
SRS CS	$34.50	$43.75		$
SRS 1	5.00	6.35		
SRS 2	5.00	6.35		
SRS 3	5.00	6.35		
SRS 4	5.00	6.35		
SRS 5	5.00	6.35		
SRS 6	5.00	6.35		
Subtotal				
Sales tax *6% for orders delivered in California or British Columbia*				
Postage *7% in Canada; overseas residents see "How to Order by Mail"*				
10% optional first-class shipping and handling *U.S. residents only*				
Gift to Insight for Living *Tax-deductible in the U.S. and Canada*				
Total amount due *Please do not send cash.*				$

If there is a balance: ☐ apply it as a donation   ☐ please refund

Form of payment:

☐ Check or money order made payable to Insight for Living

☐ Credit card (circle one):   Visa   MasterCard

Card Number _____   Expiration Date _____

Signature _____
We cannot process your credit card purchase without your signature.

Name _____

Address _____

City _____

State/Province_____   Zip/Postal Code _____

Country _____

Telephone ( )_____   Radio Station ___ ___ ___ ___
If questions arise concerning your order, we may need to contact you.

Mail this order form to the Sales Department at one of these addresses:
Insight for Living, Post Office Box 4444, Fullerton, CA 92634
Insight for Living Ministries, Post Office Box 2510, Vancouver, BC, Canada V6B 3W7